Samuel Rowbotham

ZETETIC ASTRONOMY: EARTH NOT A GLOBE!

[*Entered at Stationer's Hall.*]

ZETETIC ASTRONOMY.

EARTH NOT A GLOBE!

AN EXPERIMENTAL INQUIRY

INTO THE

TRUE FIGURE OF THE EARTH:

PROVING IT A PLANE,

WITHOUT AXIAL OR ORBITAL MOTION;

AND THE

ONLY MATERIAL WORLD

IN

THE UNIVERSE!

BY "PARALLAX."

London:
SIMPKIN, MARSHALL, AND CO., STATIONERS' HALL COURT.

Bath:
S HAYWARD, GREEN STREET.

1865.

[*The Right of Translation is Reserved by the Author.*]

ISBN: 978-1-6673-0439-7 paperback
ISBN: 978-1-6673-0440-3 hardcover

GENERAL CONTENTS

I.	Introduction – Experiments proving the Earth to be a Plane	7
II.	The Earth no Axial or Orbital Motion	36
III.	The true distance of the Sun and Stars	40
IV.	The Sun moves in a Circle over the Earth, concentric with the North Pole	42
V.	Diameter of Sun's path constantly changing	43
VI.	Cause of Day and Night, Seasons, &c.	45
VII.	Cause of "Sun rise" and "Sun set"	48
VIII.	Cause of Sun appearing larger when "Arising" and "Setting" than when on the Meridian	49
IX.	Cause of Solar and Lunar Eclipses	50
X.	Cause of Tides	57
XI.	Constitution, Condition, and ultimate Destruction of the Earth by Fire	60
XII.	Miscellanea – Moon's Phases – Moon's appearance – Planet Neptune – Pendulum Experiments as Proofs of Earth's motion	65
XIII.	Perspective on the Sea	79
XIV.	General Summary – Application – "CUI BONO"	88

SECTION I. Introduction – Experiments proving the Earth to be a Plane

ZETETIC ASTRONOMY.

THE term "zetetic" is derived from the Greek verb *zeteo;* which means to search or examine – to proceed only by inquiry. None can doubt that by making special experiments and collecting manifest and undeniable facts, arranging them in logical order, and observing what is naturally and fairly deducible, the result will be far more consistent and satisfactory than by framing a theory or system and assuming the existence of causes for which there is no direct evidence, and which can only be admitted "for the sake of argument" All theories are of this character – "supposing instead of inquiring, imagining systems instead of learning from observation and experience the true constitution of things. Speculative men, by the force of genius may invent systems that will perhaps be greatly admired for a time; these, however, are phantoms which the force of truth will sooner or later dispel ; and while we are pleased with the deceit, true philosophy, with all the arts and improvements that depend upon it, suffers. The real state of things escapes our observation ; or, if it presents itself to us, we are apt either to reject it wholly as fiction, or, by new efforts of a vain ingenuity to interweave it with our own conceits, and labour to make it tally with our favourite schemes. Thus, by blending together parts so ill-suited, the whole comes forth an absurd composition of truth and error. * * These have not done near so much harm as that pride and ambition which has led philosophers to think it beneath them to offer anything less to the world than a complete and finished system of nature ; and, in order to obtain this at once, to take the liberty of inventing certain principles and hypotheses, from which they pretend to explain all her mysteries."*

Copernicus admitted, "It is not necessary that hypotheses should be true, or even probable ; it is sufficient that they lead to results of calculation which agree with calculations. * * Neither let any one, so far as hypotheses are concerned, expect anything *certain* from astronomy ; since that science can afford nothing of the kind ; lest, in case he should adopt for truth things feigned for another purpose, he should leave this study more foolish than he came. * * The hypothesis of the terrestrial motion was *nothing but an hypothesis,* valuable only so far as it explained phenomena, and not considered with reference to absolute truth or falsehood." The Newtonian and all other "systems of nature" are little better than the "hypothesis of the terrestrial motion" of Copernicus. The foundations or premises are always unproved ; no proof is ever attempted ; the necessity for it is denied ; it is considered sufficient that the assumptions shall *seem* to explain the phenomena selected In this way it is that one theory supplants another ; that system gives way to system as one failure after another compels opinions to change. This will ever be so ; there will always exist in the mind a degree of uncertainty ; a disposition to look upon philosophy as a vain pretension; a something almost antagonistic to the highest aspirations in which humanity can indulge, unless the practice of theorising be given up, and the method of simple inquiry, the "zetetic" process be adopted "Nature speaks to us in a peculiar language ; in the language of phenomena, she answers at all times the questions which are put to her ; and such questions are experiments."* Not experiments only which corroborate what has previously been *assumed* to be true; but experiments in every form bearing on the subject of inquiry, before a conclusion is drawn or premises affirmed.

We have an excellent example of zetetic reasoning in an arithmetical operation ; more especially so in what is called the "Golden Rule," or the "Rule-of-Three." If one hundred weight of any article is worth a given sum, what will some other weight of that article be worth ? The separate figures may be considered as the elements or facts of the inquiry ; the placing and working of these as the logical arrangement ; and the quotient or answer as the fair and natural deduction. Hence, in every zetetic process, the conclusion arrived at is essentially a quotient, which, if the details be correct, must, of necessity, be true beyond the reach or power of contradiction.

In our courts of Justice we have also an example of the zetetic process. A prisoner is placed at the bar ; evidence for and against him is advanced ; it is carefully arranged and patiently considered ; and only such a verdict given as could not in justice be avoided. Society would not tolerate any other procedure ; it would brand with infamy whoever should assume a prisoner to be guilty, and prohibit all evidence but such as would corroborate the assumption. Yet such is the character of theoretical philosophy !

The zetetic process is also the natural method of investigation; nature herself teaches it. Children invariably seek information by asking questions – by earnestly inquiring from those around them. Question after question in rapid and exciting succession will often proceed from a child, until the most profound in learning and philosophy will feel puzzled to reply. If then both nature and justice, as well as the common sense and practical experience of mankind demand, and will not be content with less or other than the zetetic process, why should it he ignored and violated by the learned in philosophy? Let the practice of theorising be cast aside as one fetal to the full development of truth ; oppressive to the reasoning power; and in every sense inimical to the progress and permanent improvement of the human race.

If then we adopt the zetetic process to ascertain the true figure and condition of the Earth, we shall find that instead of its being a globe, and moving in space, it is the directly contrary – A Plane ; without motion, and unaccompanied by anything in the Firmament analogous to itself.

If the Earth is a globe, and 25,000 miles in circumference, the surface of all standing water must have a certain degree of convexity – every part must be an arc of a circle, curvating from the summit at the rate of 8 inches per mile multiplied by the square of the distance. That this may be sufficiently understood, the following quotation is given from the *Encyclopædia. Britannica,* art. "Levelling." "If a line which crosses the plumb-line at right

SECTION I. Introduction – Experiments proving the Earth to be a Plane

angles be continued for any considerable length it will rise above the Earth's surface (the Earth being globular) ; and this rising will be as the square of the distance to which the said right line is produced ; that is to say, it is raised eight inches very nearly above the Earth's surface at one mile's distance ; four times as much, or 32 inches, at the distance of two miles; nine times as much, or 72 inches, at the distance of three miles. This is owing to the globular figure of the Earth, and this rising is the difference between the true and apparent levels ; the curve of the Earth being the true level, and the tangent to it the apparent level. So soon does the difference between the true and apparent levels become perceptible that it is necessary to make an allowance for it if the distance betwixt the two stations exceeds two chains.

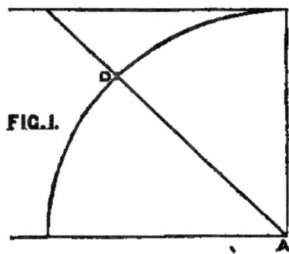

FIG.1.

Let B. D. be a small portion of the Earth's circumference, whose centre of curvature is A. and consequently all the points of this arc will be on a level. But a tangent B. C. meeting the vertical line A. D. in C. will be the apparent level at the point B. and therefore D. C. is the difference between the apparent and the true level at the point B.

The distance C. D. must be deducted from the observed height to have the true difference of level ; or the differences between the distances of two points from the surface of the Earth or from the centre of curvature A. But we shall afterwards see how this correction may be avoided altogether in certain cases. To find an expression for C. D. we have Euclid, third book, 36 prop. which proves that B C^2 = C. D. *(2 A D × C D);* but since in all cases of levelling C. D. is exceedingly small compared with 2 A. D., we may safely neglect C. D^2 and then B C^2 = 2 A. D × C. D. or C. D = $\frac{B.C^2}{2\,A.D.}$ Hence the depression of the true level is equal to the square of the distance divided by twice the radius of the curvature of the Earth.

For example, taking a distance of four miles, the square of 4 = 16, and putting down twice the radius of the Earth's curvature as in round figures about 8000 miles, we make the depression on four miles = $\frac{16}{8000}$ of a mile = $\frac{16 \times 1760}{8000}$ yards = $\frac{176}{50}$ yards = $\frac{528}{50}$ feet, or rather better than 10½ feet.

Or, if we take the mean radius of the Earth as the mean radius of its curvature, and consequently 2 A. D = 7,912 miles, then 5,280 feet being 1 mile, we shall have C. D. the depression in inches $= \frac{5280 \times 12 \times B\ C^2}{7912} = 8008$ B.C^2 inches.

The preceding remarks suppose the visual ray C. B. to be a straight line, whereas on account of the unequal densities of the air at different distances from the Earth, the rays of light are incurvated by refraction. The effect of this is to lessen the difference between the true and apparent levels, but in such an extremely variable and uncertain manner that if any constant or fixed allowance is made for it in formulæ or tables, it will often lead to a greater error than what it was intended to obviate. For though the refraction may at a mean compensate for about a seventh of the curvature of the earth, it sometimes exceeds a fifth, and at other times does not amount to a fifteenth. We have, therefore, made no allowance for refraction in the foregone formulæ."

If the Earth is a globe, there cannot be a question that, however irregular the *land* may be in form, the *water* must have a convex surface. And as the difference between the true and apparent level, or the degree of curvature would be 8 inches in one mile, and in every succeeding mile 8 inches multiplied by the square of the distance, there can he no difficulty in detecting either its actual existence or proportion. Experiments made upon the sea have been objected to on account of its constantly-changing altitude ; and the existence of banks and channels which produce a "a crowding" of the waters, currents, and other irregularities. Standing water has therefore been selected, and many important experiments have been made, the most simple of which is the following : – In the county of Cambridge there is an artificial river or canal, called the "Old Bedford." It is upwards of twenty miles long, and passes in a straight line through that part of the fens called the "Bedford level." The water is nearly stationery – often entirely so, and throughout its entire length has no interruption from locks or water-gates ; so that it is in every respect well adapted for ascertaining whether any and what amount of convexity really exists. A boat with a flag standing three feet above the water, was directed to sail from a place called "Welney Bridge," to another place called "Welche's Dam." These two points are six statute miles apart. The observer, with a good telescope, was seated in the water as a bather (it being the summer season), with the eye not exceeding eight inches above the surface. The flag and the boat down to the water's edge were clearly *visible throughout the whole distance !* From this observation it was concluded that the water did not decline to any degree from the line of sight ; whereas the water would be 6 feet higher in the centre of the arc of 6 miles extent than at the two places Bridge and Welche's Dam ; but as the eye of the observer was only eight inches above the water, the highest point of the surface would he at one mile from the place of observation ; below which point the surface of the water at the end of the remaining five miles would he 16 feet 8 inches ($5^2 \times 8 = 200$ inches). This will be rendered clear by the following diagram : –

SECTION I. Introduction – Experiments proving the Earth to be a Plane

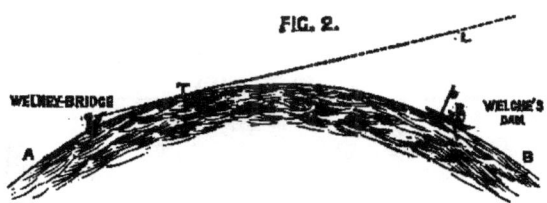

FIG. 2.

Let A B represent the arc of water from Welney Bridge to Welche's Dam, six miles in length; and A L the line of sight, which is now a tangent to the arc A B ; the point of contact, T, is 1 mile from the eye of the observer at A ; and from T to the boat at B is 5 miles ; the square of 5 miles multiplied by 8 inches is 200 inches, or, in other words, that the boat at B would have been 200 inches or above 16 feet below the surface of the water at T ; and the flag on the boat, which was 3 feet high, would have been 13 feet below the line-of-sight, ATL!!

From this experiment it follows that the surface of standing water is *not convex,* and therefore *that the Earth* is not A GLOBE! On the Contrary, this simple experiment is all-sufficient to prove that the surface of the water is parallel to the line-of-sight, and is therefore horizontal, and that the Earth c*annot* be other than A PLANE! In diagram Figure 3 this is perfectly illustrated.

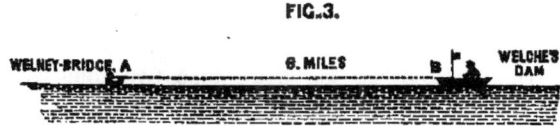

FIG. 3.

A B is the line-of-sight, and C D the surface of the water equidistant from or parallel to it throughout the whole distance observed.

Although, on account of the variable state of the water, objections have been raised to experiments made upon the sea-shore to test the convexity of the flood or ebb-tide level, none can be urged against observations made from higher altitudes. For example, – the distance across the Irish Sea between Douglas Harbour, in the Isle of Man, and the Great Orm's Head in North Wales is 60 miles. If the earth is a globe, the surface of the water would form an arc 60 miles in length, the centre of which would be 1,944 feet higher than the coast line at either end, so that an observer would be obliged to attain this altitude before he could see the Welsh coast from the Isle of Man : as shown in the diagram, Figure 4.

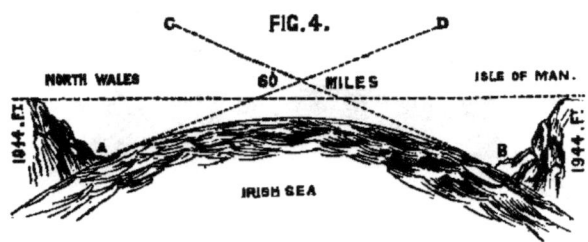

It is well known, however, that from an altitude not exceeding 100 feet the Great Orm's Head is visible in clear weather from Douglas Harbour. The altitude of 100 feet could cause the line of sight to touch the horizon at the distance of nearly 13 miles ; and from the horizon to Orm's Head being 47 miles, the square of this number multiplied by 8 inches gives 1472 feet as the distance which the Welsh coast line would be below the line of sight B C. – A representing the Great Orm's Head, which, being 600 feet high, its summit would he 872 feet below the horizon.

Many similar experiments have been made across St. Georges Channel, between points near Dublin and Holyhead, and always with results entirely incompatible with the doctrine of rotundity.

Again, it is known that the horizon at sea, whatever distance it may extend to the right and left of the observer on land, always appears as a straight line. The following experiment has been tried in various parts of the country. At Brighton, on a rising ground near the race course, two poles were fixed in the earth six yards apart, and directly opposite the sea. Between these poles a line was tightly stretched parallel to the distant horizon. From the centre of the line the view embraced not less than 20 miles on each side, making a distance of 40 miles A vessel was observed sailing directly westwards ; the line cut the rigging a little above the bulwarks, which it did for several hours or until the vessel had sailed the whole distance of 40 miles. This will be understood by reference to the diagram, Figure 5.

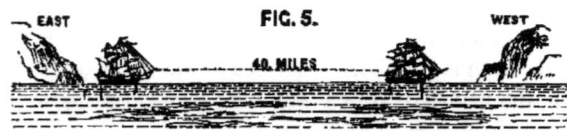

If the Earth were a globe, the appearance would be as represented in Figure 6.

SECTION I. Introduction – Experiments proving the Earth to be a Plane

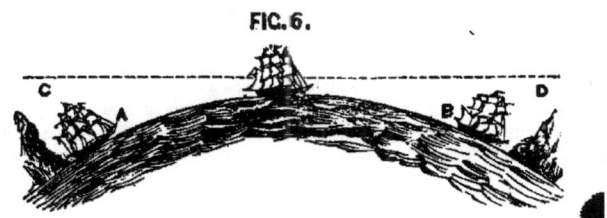

The ship coming into view from the east would have to ascend an inclined plane for 20 miles until it arrived at the centre of the are A B, whence it would have to descend for the same distance. The square of 20 miles multiplied by 8 inches gives 266 feet as the amount the vessel would he below the line C D at the beginning and at the end of the 40 miles.

If we stand upon the deck of a ship, or mount to the mast head ; or go to the top of a mountain, or ascend above the Earth in a balloon, and look over the sea, the surface appears as a vast inclined plane rising up until in the distance it intercepts the line of sight If a good mirror be held in the opposite direction, the horizon will he reflected as a well-defined mark or line across the centre, as represented in diagram, Figure 7.

Ascending or descending, the distant horizon does the same. It rises and falls with the observer, and is always on a level with his eye. If he takes a position where the water surrounds him – as at the mast-head of a ship out of sight of land, or on the summit of a small island far from the mainland, the surface of the sea appears to rise up on all sides equally and to surround him like the walls of an immense amphitheatra. He seems to be in the centre of a large concavity, the edges of which expand or contract as he takes a higher or lower position. This appearance is so well known to sea-going travellers that nothing more need be said in its support But the appearance from a balloon is familiar only to a small number of observers, and therefore it will be useful to quote from those who have written upon the subject

"*The Apparent Concavity of the Earth as seen from a Balloon.* – A perfectly-formed circle encompassed the visible planisphere beneath, or rather the concavo-sphere it might now be called, for I had attained a height from which the surface of the Earth assumed a regularly hollowed or concave appearance – an optical illusion which increases as you recede from it. At the greatest elevation I attained, which was about a mile-and-a-half, the appearance of the World around me assumed a shape or form like that which is made by placing two watch-glasses together by their edges, the balloon apparently in the central cavity all the time of its flight at that elevation." – *Wise's Aeronautics.*

"Another curious effect of the aerial ascent was, that the Earth, when we were at our greatest altitude, positively appeared *concave,* looking like a huge dark bowl, rather than the convex sphere such as we naturally expect to see it. * * * The horizon always appears to be on a level with our eye, and seems to rise as we rise, until at length the elevation of the circular boundary line of the sight becomes so marked that the Earth assumes the anomalous appearance as we have said of a *concave* rather than a *convex* body." – *Mayhem's Great World of London.*

Mr. Elliott, an American æronaut, in a letter giving an account of his ascension from Baltimore, thus speaks of the appearance of the Earth from a balloon : –

"I don't know that I ever hinted heretofore that the æronaut may well be the most sceptical man about the rotundity of the Earth. Philosophy imposes the truth upon us ; but the view of the Earth from the elevation of a balloon is that of an immense terrestial basin, the deeper part of which is that directly under one's feet. As we ascend, the Earth beneath us seems to recede – actually to sink away – while the horizon gradually and gracefully lifts a diversified slope stretching away farther and farther to aline that, at the highest elevation, seems to close with the sky. Thus upon a clear day, the æronaut feels as if suspended at about an equal distance between the vast blue oceanic concave above, and the equally expanded terrestial basin below."

"The chief peculiarity of the view from a balloon, at a considerable elevation, was the altitude of the horizon, which remained practically on a level with the eye at an elevation of two miles, causing the surface of the Earth to appear *concave* instead of *convex*, and to recede during the rapid ascent, whilst the horizon and the balloon seemed to be stationary." – *London Journal*, July 18, 1857.

During the important balloon ascents recently made for scientific purposes by Mr. Coxwell and Mr. Glaisher, of the Royal Greenwich Observatory, the same phenomenon was observed –

"The horizon always appeared on a level with the car." – Vide "Glaisher's Report."

The following diagram represents this appearance : –

SECTION I. Introduction – Experiments proving the Earth to be a Plane

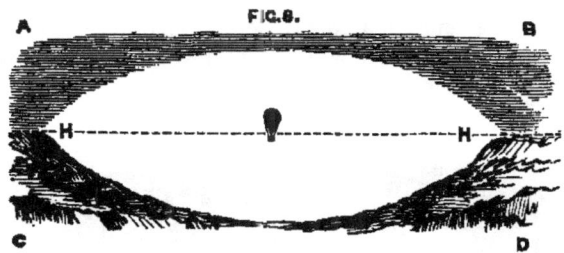

The surface of the earth C D appears to rise to the line-of-sight from the balloon, and "seems to close with the sky" at the points H H in the same manner that the ceiling and the floor of a long room, or the top and bottom of a tunnel appear to approach each other, and from the same cause, viz. : that they are *parallel to the line-of-sight, and therefore horizontal.*

If the Earth's surface were convex the observer, looking from a balloon, instead of seeing it gradually ascend to the level of the eye, would have to look downwards to the horizon H H, as represented in figure 10, and the amount of dip

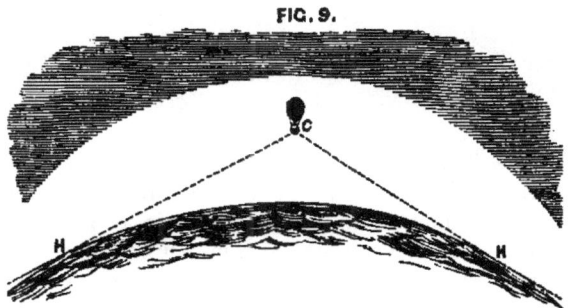

in the line-of-sight C H would be the greatest at the highest elevation.

Many more experiments have been made than are here described, but the selection now given is amply sufficient to prove that the surface of water is horizontal, and that the Earth, taken as a whole, its land and water together, is not a globe, has really no degree of sphericity ; but is "to all intents and purposes" A plane !

If we now consider the fact that when we travel by land or sea, and from any part of the known world, in a direction towards the North polar star, we shall arrive at one and the same point, we are forced to the conclusion that what has hitherto been called the North Polar region, is really the Centre of the Earth. That from this northern centre the land diverges and stretches out, of necessity, towards a circumference, which must now be called the Southern Region :

which is a vast circle, and not a pole or centre. That there is One Centre – the North, and One Circumference – the South. This language will be better understood by reference to the diagram Figure 10.

FIG. 10.

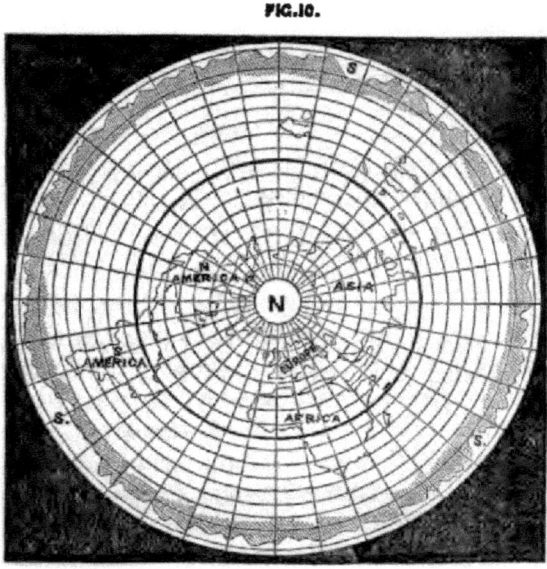

N represents the northern centre ; and S S S the southern circumference – both icy or frozen regions. That the south is an immense ring, or glacial boundary, is evident from the fact, that within the antarctic circle the most experienced, scientific, and daring navigators have failed in their attempts to sail, in a direct manner, completely round it Lieut. Wilkes, of the American Navy, after great and prolonged efforts, and much confusion in his reckoning, and seeing no prospect of success, was obliged to give up his attempt and return to the north. This he acknowledged in a letter to Captain Sir James Clarke Ross, with whose intention to explore the south seas he had become acquainted, in which the following words occur : "I hope you intend to circumnavigate the antarctic circle. I made 70 degrees of it." Captain Ross, however, was himself greatly confused in his attempts to navigate the southern region. In his account of the voyage he says, at page 96 – "We found ourselves every day from 12 to 16 miles by observation in advance of our reckoning." "By our observations we found ourselves 58 miles to the eastward of our reckoning in two days." And in this and other ways all the great navigators have been frustrated in their efforts, and have been more or less confounded in their attempts to sail round the Earth upon or beyond the antarctic circle. But if the southern region is a pole or centre, like the north, there would be little difficulty in circumnavigating it, for the distance

SECTION I. Introduction – Experiments proving the Earth to be a Plane

round would be comparatively small When it is seen that the Earth is not a sphere, but a plane, having only one centre, the north ; and that the south is the vast icy boundary of the world, the difficulties experienced by circumnavigators can be easily understood.

Having given a surface or bird's-eye view of the Earth, the following sectional representation will aid in completing the description.

FIG. II.

E E represents the Earth; W W the "great deep," or the waters which surround the land ; N the northern centre; and S S sections of the southern ice. As the present description is purely zetetic, and as every fact must therefore have its fullest value assigned to it, and its consequences represented, a peculiarity must be pointed out in the foregoing diagram. It will be observed that from about the points E E the surface of the water *rises* towards the south S S. It is clearly ascertained that the altitude of the water in various parts of the world is much influenced by the pressure of the atmosphere – however this pressure is caused – and it is well known that the atmospheric pressure in the south is constantly less than it is in the north, and therefore the water in the southern region must always be considerably higher than it is in the northern. Hence the peculiarity referred to in the diagram. The following quotation from Sir James Ross's voyages, p. 483, will corroborate the above statements : – "Our barometrical experiments appear to prove that a gradual diminution of atmospheric pressure occurs as we proceed southwards from the tropic of Capricorn. * * * It has hitherto been considered that the mean pressure of the atmosphere at the level of the sea was nearly the same in all parts of the world, as no material difference occurs between the equator and the highest northern latitudes. * * * The causes of the atmospheric pressure being so *very much less* in the southern than in the northern hemispheres remains to be determined."

Thus, putting all theories aside, we have seen that direct experiment demonstrates the important truth, *that the Earth is an extended Plane.* Literally, "Stretched out upon the waters;" "Founded on the seas and established on the floods;" "Standing in the water and out of the water." How far the southern icy region extends horizontally, or how deep the waters upon and in which the earth stands or is supported are questions which cannot yet be answered. In Zetetic philosophy the foundation must be well secured, progress must be made step by step, making good the ground as we proceed ; and whenever a difficulty presents itself, or evidence fails to carry us farther, we must promptly and candidly acknowledge it, and prepare for future investigation ; but never fill up the inquiry by theory and assumption. In the present instance there is no practical evidence as to the extent of the southern ice and the "great deep." Who shall say whether the depth and extent of the "mighty waters" *have* a limit, or constitute the "World without end ?"

Having advanced direct and special evidence that the surface of the earth is not convex, but, on the contrary, a vast and irregular plane, it now becomes important that the leading phenomena upon which the doctrine of rotundity has been founded should be carefully examined. First, it is contended that because the hull of an outward-bound vessel disappears before the mast head, the water is convex, and therefore the Earth is a globe. In this conclusion, however, there is an assumption involved, viz., that such a phenomenon *can only* result from a convex surface. Inquiry will show that this is erroneous. If we select for observation a few miles of straight and level railway, we shall find that the rails, which are parallel, appear in the distance to approach each other. But the two rails which are nearest together do so more rapidly than those which are farthest asunder, as shown in the following diagram, Figure 12.

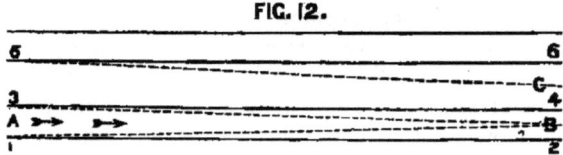

Let the observer stand at the point A, looking in the direction of the arrows ; and the rails 1.2 3.4. will appear to join at the point B, but the rail 5.6 will appear to have converged only as fer as C towards B.

Again, let a train be watched from the point A in Figure 13.

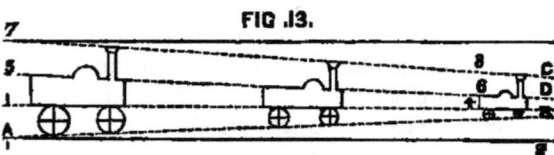

The observer looking from A, with his eye midway between the bottom of the carriage and the rail, will see the diameter of the wheels gradually diminish as they receda The lines 1.2 and 1.4 will appear to approach each other until at the point B they will come together, and the space, including the wheels, between the bottom of the carriage and the rail will there disappear. The floor of the carriage will seem to be sliding without wheels upon the rail 1.2; but the lines 5.6 and 7.8 will yet have converged only to C and D.

The same phenomenon may be observed with a long row of lamps, where

SECTION I. Introduction – Experiments proving the Earth to be a Plane

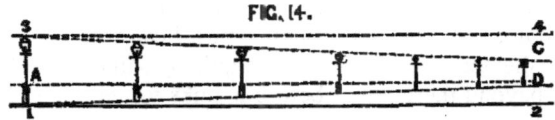

FIG. 14.

The lines 1.2 and A D will converge at the point D and the pedestal of the lamp at D will seem to have disappeared, but the line 3.4, which represents the true altitude of the lamps, will only have converged to the point C.

A narrow bank running along the side of a straight portion of railway, upon which poles are placed for supporting the wires of the electric telegraph will produce the same appearance, as shown in Figure 15.

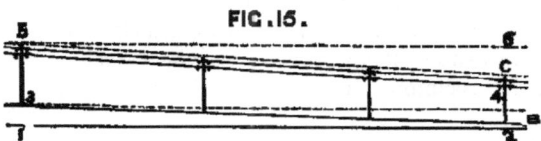

FIG. 15.

The bank having the altitude 1.3 and 2.4 will, in the distance of two or three miles (according to its depth) disappear to the eye of an observer placed at Figure 1 ; and the telegraph pole at Figure 2 will seem not to stand upon a bank at all, but upon the actual railway. The line 3.4 will merge into the line 1.2 at the point B, while the line 5.6 will only have descended to the position C.

Many other familiar instances could be given to show the true law of perspective; which is, that parallel lines appear in the distance to converge to one and the same datum line, but to reach it at different distances if themselves dissimilarly distant This law being remembered, it is easy to understand how the hull of an outward-bound ship, although sailing upon a plane surface disappears before the mast-head In Figure 16, let A B represent the surface of the water; C H the line of sight ; and E D the altitude of the mast-head. Then, as A B and C H are

FIG. 16.

nearer to each other than A B and E D, they will converge and appear to meet at the point H, which is the practical, or, as it would be better to call it, the *optical* horizon The hull of the vessel being contained within the lines A B and C H, must gradually diminish as these converge, until at H, or the horizon, it enters the vanishing point and disappears; but the mast-head represented by the line E D is still *above* the horizon at H. and will require to sail more or less, according to its altitude, beyond the point H before it sinks to the line C H, or, in other words, before the lines A B and E D form the same angle as A B and C H.

It will be evident also that should the elevation of the observer be greater than at C, the horizon or vanishing point would not be formed at H, but at a greater distance ; and therefore the hull of the vessel would be longer visible. Or, if, when the hull has disappeared at H, the observer ascends from the elevation at C to a higher position nearer to E, it will again be seen. Thus all these phenomena which have so long been considered as proofs of the Earth's rotundity are really optical sequences of the contrary doctrine. To argue that because the lower part of an outward-bound ship disappears before the highest the water must be round, is to *assume* that a *round* surface *ordy* can produce this effect ! But it is now shown that a *plane* surface *necessarily* produces this effect ; and therefore the assumption is not required, and the argument involved is fallacious !

It may here be observed that no help can be given to this doctrine of rotundity by quoting the prevailing theory of perspective. The law represented in the foregoing diagrams is the "law of nature." It may be seen in every layer of a long wall, in every hedge and bank of the roadside, and indeed in every direction where lines and objects run parallel to each other ; but no illustration of the contrary perspective is ever to be seen ! except in the distorted pictures, otherwise cleverly and beautifully drawn as they are, which abound in our public and private collections.

The theory which" affirms that parallel lines converge only to one and the same point upon the eye-line is an error. It is true only of lines equidistant from the eye-line. It is true that parallel lines converge to one and the same *eye-line*, but *meet it at different distances when more or less apart from each other.* This is the true law of perspective as shown by Nature herself; any other idea is fallacious and will deceive whoever may hold and apply it to practice.

As it is of great importance that the difference should be clearly understood, the following diagram is given. Let E L (Figure 17) represent the eye-line and C the vanishing point of

SECTION I. Introduction – Experiments proving the Earth to be a Plane

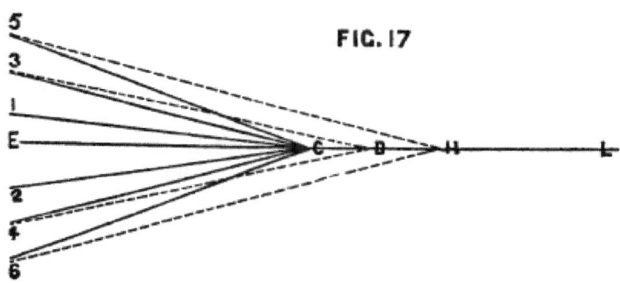

FIG. 17

thelines, 1 C 2 C; then the lines 3.4.5.6, although converging *somewhere* to the line E L, will not do so to the point C, but 3 and 4 will proceed to D and 5 and 6 to H. It is repeated, that lines *equidistant* from the *datum* will converge on the *same point* and at the *same distance;* but lines *not* equidistant will converge on the same *datum* but at *different distances* ! A very good illustration of the difference is given in Figure 18. Theoretic perspective would bring

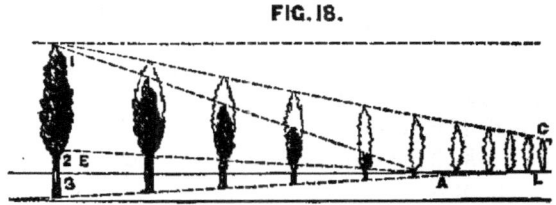

FIG. 18.

the lines 1, 2, and 3 to the same *datum* line E L and to the *same point* A But the true or natural law would bring the lines 2 and 3 to the point A because equidistant from the eye-line E L ; but the line 1 being farther from E L than either 2 or 3, would be taken beyond the point A on towards C, until it formed the *same angle* upon the line E L as 2 and 3 form at the point A.

The subject of perspective will not be rendered sufficiently clear unless an explanation be given of the cause and character of what is technically called the "vanishing point." Why do objects, even when raised above the earth, vanish at a given distance ? It is known, and can easily be proved by experiment, that "the range of the eye, or diameter of the field of vision is 110° ; consequently this is the *largest* angle under which an object can be seen. The range of vision is from 110° to 1.° * * The *smallest* angle under which an object can be seen is upon an average for different sights the 60th part of a degree, or *one minute* in space ; so that when an object is removed from the eye 3000 times its own diameter, it will only just be distinguishable; consequently, the greatest distance at which we can behold an object, like a shilling, of an inch in diameter is 3000 inches or 250 feet"* It may, therefore, be very easily understood that a line passing over the hull of a ship, and continuing parallel to the surface of the water, must converge to the vanishing point at the distance of about 3000 times its own elevation ; in other words, if the surface of the hull be 10 feet above the water it will vanish at 3,000 times 10 feet ; or nearly six statute miles ; but if the mast-head be 30 feet above the water, it will be visible for 90,000 feet or over 17 miles; so that it could be seen upon the horizon for a distance of eleven miles *after the hull had entered the vanishing point !* Hence the phenomenon of a receding ship's hull being the first to disappear, which has been so universally quoted and relied upon as proving the rotundity of the Earth is fairly and logically a proof of the very contrary ! It has been misapplied in consequence of an erroneous view of the law of perspective, and the desire to support a theory. That it is valueless for such a purpose has already been shown ; and that, even if there were no question of the Earth's form involved, it could not arise from the convexity of the water, is proved by the following experiment : – Let an observer stand upon the sea-shore with the eye at an elevation of about six feet above the water, and watch a vessel until it is just "hull down." If now a good telescope be applied the hull will be distinctly *restored to sight!* From which it must be concluded that it had disappeared through the influence of perspective, and not from having sunk behind the summit of a convex surface ! Had it done so it would follow that the telescope had either carried the line-of-sight through the mass of water, or over its surface and down the other side ! But the power of "looking round a corner" or penetrating a dense and extensive medium has never yet been attributed to such an instrument ! If the elevation of the observer be much greater than six feet the distance at which the vanishing point is formed will be so great that the telescope may not have power enough to magnify or enlarge the angle constituting it ; when the experiment would appear to fail. But the failure would only be apparent, for a telescope of sufficient power to magnify at the horizon or vanishing point would certainly restore the hull at the greater distance.

An illustration or proof of the Earth's rotundity is also supposed to be found in the fact that navigators by sailing due east or west return in the opposite direction. Here, again, a supposition is involved, viz., that upon a globe *only* could this occur. But it is easy to prove that it could take place as perfectly upon a circular plane as upon a sphere. Let it first be clearly understood what is really meant by sailing *due east and west.* Practically it is sailing at right angles to north and south : this is determined ordinarily by the mariners' compass, but more accurately by the meridian lines which converge to the northern centre of the Earth. Bearing this in mind, let N in Figure 19 represent the northern centre ;

SECTION I. Introduction – Experiments proving the Earth to be a Plane

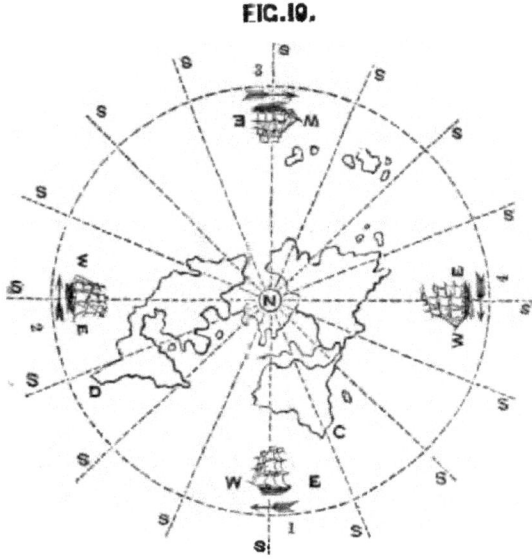

FIG.10.

and the lines N. S. the directions north and south. Then let the small arrow, Figure 1, represent a vessel on the meridian of Greenwich, with its head W. at right angles, or due west ; and the stem E. due east It is evident that in passing to the position of the arrow, Figure 2, which is still due west or square to the meridian, the arc 1.2 must be described; and in sailing still farther under the same condition, the arcs 2.3, 3.4, and 4.1 will be successively passed over until the meridian of Greenwich, Figure 1, is arrived at, which was the point of departure. Thus a mariner, by keeping the head of his vessel due west, or at right angles to the north and south, practically circumnavigates a plane surface ; or, in other words, he describes a circle *upon a plane*, at a greater or lesser distance from the centre N, and being at all times square to the radii north and south, he is *compelled* to do so – *because* the earth is a plane, having a central region, towards which the compass and the meridian lines which guide him, converge. So far, then, from the fact of a vessel sailing due west coming home from the east, and *vice versa*, being a proof of the earth's rotundity, it is simply a phenomenon, consistent with and dependent upon its being a plane ! The subject may be perfectly illustrated by the following simple experiment : – Take a round table, fix a pin in the centre ; to this attach a thread, and extend it to the edge. Call the centre the north and the circumference the south; then, at any distance between the centre and the circumference, a direction at right angles to the thread will be due east and west; and a small object, as a pencil, placed across or square to the thread, to represent a ship, may be carried completely round the table without its right-angled position being altered; or, the right-angled position firmly maintained, the vessel must of necessity describe a circle on being moved from right to left or left to right. Referring again to the diagram, Figure 19, the vessel may sail from the north towards the south, upon the meridian Figure 1, and there turning due west, may pass Cape Horn, represented by D, and continue its westerly course until it passes the point C, or the Cape of *Good* Hope, and again reaches the meridian, Figure 1, upon which it may return to the north Those, then, who hold that the earth is a globe because it can be circumnavigated, have an argument which is logically incomplete and fallacious. This will be seen at once by putting it in the syllogistic form : –

A globe *only* can be circumnavigated :
The Earth has been circumnavigated :
Therefore the Earth is a globe.

It has been shown that a *plane* can be circumnavigated, and therefore the first or major proposition is false ; and, being so, the conclusion is false. This portion of the subject furnishes a striking instance of the necessity of, at all times, proving a proposition by direct and immediate evidence, instead of quoting a natural phenomenon as a proof of what has previously been assumed. But a theory will not admit of this method, and therefore the zetetic process, or inquiry before conclusion, entirely eschewing assumption, is the only course which can lead to simple and unalterable truth. Whoever creates or upholds a theory, adopts a monster which will sooner or later betray and enslave him, or make him ridiculous in the eyes of practical observers.

Closely following the subject of circumnavigation, the gain and loss of time discovered on sailing east and west is referred to as another proof of rotundity. But this illustration is equally fallacious with the last, and from the same cause, viz., the assumption that a *globe only* could produce the effect observed. It will be seen, by reference to diagram, Figure 19, that the effect must take place equally upon a plane as upon a globe. Let the ship, W E, upon the meridian, Figure 1, at 12 at noon, begin to sail towards the position, Figure 2, which it will reach the next day at 12, or in 24 hours: the sun during the same 24 hours will have returned only to Figure 1, and will require to move for another hour or more until it reaches the ship at Figure 2, making 25 hours instead of 24, in which the sun would have returned to the ship, if it had remained at Figure 1. In this way, the sun is more and more behind the meridian time of the ship, as it proceeds day after day upon its westerly course, so that on completing the circumnavigation the ship's time is a day later than the solar time, reckoning to and from the meridian of Greenwich. But the contrary follows if the ship sails from Figure I towards Figure 4, or the east, because it will meet the sun one hour earlier than the 24 hours which would be required for it to pass on to Figure 1. Hence, on completing the circle 1.4.3.2.1, the time at the ship would be one day in advance of the time at Greenwich, or the position Figure 1. Captain Sir J. C. Boss, at page 132, vol. 2, says – "November 25, having by sailing to the

SECTION I. Introduction – Experiments proving the Earth to be a Plane

eastward gained 12 hours, it became necessary, on crossing the 180th degree and entering upon west longitude, in order to have our time correspond with that of England, to have two days following of the same date, and by this means lose the time we had gained, and still were gaining, as we sailed to the eastward."

In further illustration of this matter, and to impress the mind of the readers with its importance as an evidence in support of the theory of the earth's sphericity, several authors have given the following story : – Two brothers, twins, born within a few minutes of each other, and therefore of the same age, on growing to manhood went to sea. They both circumnavigated the earth, but in opposite directions ; and when they again met, one was a day older than the other !

Whatever truth there may be in this account, it is here shown to be no more favourable to the idea of rotundity than it is to the opposite fact that the earth is a plane ; as both forms will permit of the same effect

Another phenomenon supposed to prove rotundity, is found in the fect that Polaris, or the north polar star, gradually sinks to the horizon as the mariner approaches the equator, on passing which it becomes invisible. First, it is an ordinary effect of perspective for an object to appear lower and lower as the observer recedes. Let any one try the experiment of looking at a lighthouse, church spire, monument, gas-lamp, or other elevated object, from the distance of a few yards, and notice the angle at which it is observed : on going farther away, the angle will diminish and the object appear lower, until, if the distance be sufficiently great, the line-of-sight to the object, and the apparently ascending surface of the Earth upon which it stands will converge to the angle which constitutes the vanishing point ; at a single yard beyond which it will be invisible. This, then, is the necessary result of the everywhere visible law of perspective operating between the eye-line and the plane surface upon which the object stands ; and has no relation whatever to rotundity.

It is not denied that a similar depression of a distant object would take place upon a globe ; it is simply contended that it would not occur upon a globe exclusively. But if the Earth is a sphere and the pole star hangs over the northern axis, it would be impossible to see it for a single degree beyond the equator, or 90 degrees from the pole. The line-of-sight would become a tangent to the sphere, and consequently several thousand miles out of and divergent from the direction of the pole-star. Many cases, however, are on record of the north polar star being visible far beyond the equator, as far even as the tropic of Capricorn. In the *Times* newspaper of May 13, 1862, under the head of "Naval and Military Intelligence," it is stated that Captain Wilkins distinctly saw the Southern Cross and the polar star at midnight in 23·53 degrees of latitude, and longitude 35 46.

This would be utterly impossible if the Earth were a globe, as shown in the diagram, Figure 20.

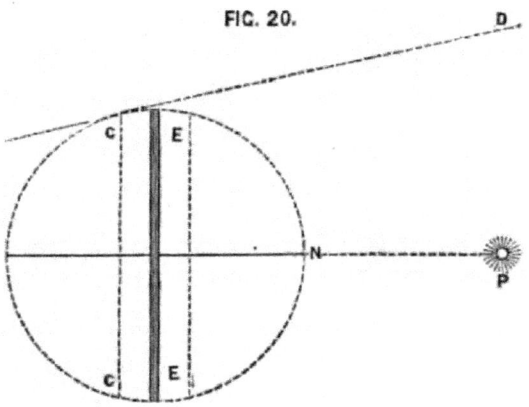

FIG. 20.

Let N represent the north pole, E E the equator, C C the tropic of Capricorn, and P the polar star. It will be evident that the line-of-sight C D being a tangent to the Earth beyond the equator E must diverge from the axis N and could not by any known possibility cause the star P to be visible to an observer at C. No matter how distant the star P, the line C D being divergent from the direction N P could never come in contact with it The fact, then, that the polar star has often been seen from *many degrees* beyond the equator, is really an important argument against the doctrine of the Earth's rotundity.

It has been thought that because a pendulum vibrates more rapidly in the northern region than at the equator, the Earth is thereby proved to be a globe ; and because the variation in the velocity is not exactly as it should be if all the surface of the Earth were equidistant from the centre, it has been concluded that the Earth is an oblate spheroid, or that its diameter is rather less through the poles than it is through the equator. The difference was calculated by Newton to be the 235th part of the whole diameter ; or that the polar was to the equatorial diameter as 689 to 692. Huygens gave the proportion as 577 to 875 or a difference of about one-third of the whole diameter. Others have given still different proportions ; but recently the difference of opinion has become so great that many have concluded that the Earth is really instead of oblate an *oblong* spheroid. It is certain that the question when attempted to be answered by measuring arcs of the meridian, is less satisfactory than was expected. This will be evident from the following quotation from the account of the ordnance survey of Great Britain, which was conducted by the Duke of Richmond, Col. Mudge, General Roy, Mr. Dalby, and others, who measured base lines on Hounslow Heath and Salisbury Plain with glass rods and steel chains : "when these were connected by a chain of triangles and the length computed the result did not differ more than one inch from the actual measurements – a convincing proof of the accuracy with which all the operations had been conducted.

SECTION I. Introduction – Experiments proving the Earth to be a Plane

The two stations, of Beachy Head in Sussex and Dunnose in the Isle of Wight, are visible from each other, and more than 64 miles asunder, nearly in a direction from east to west ; their exact distance was found by the geodetical operations to be 339,397 feet (64 miles and 1477 feet). The azimuth, or bearing of the line between them with respect to the meridian, and also the latitude of Beachy Head, were determined by astronomical observations. From these data the length of a degree perpendicular to the meridian was computed ; and this, compared with the length of a meridional degree in the same latitude, gave the proportion of the polar to the equatorial axis. The result thus obtained, however, differed considerably from that obtained by meridional degrees. It has been found impossible to explain the want of agreement in a satisfactory way. * * By comparing the celestial with the terrestial arcs, the length of degrees in various parallels was determined as in the following table : –

	Latitude of middle point. ° ′ ″	Fathoms.
Arbury Hill and Clifton	52 50 29·8	60,760
Blenheim and Clifton	52 38 56·1	60,769
Greenwich and Clifton	52 28 5·7	60,794
Dunnose and Clifton	52 2 19·8	60,820
Arbury Hill and Greenwich	51 51 4·1	60,849
Dunnose and Arbury Hill	51 35 18 2	60,864
Blenheim and Dunnose	51 13 18·2	60,890
Dunnose and Greenwich	51 2 54·2	60,884

This table presents a singular deviation from the common rule ; for instead of the degrees *increasing* as we proceed from north to south, they appear to *decrease,* as if the Earth were an *oblong* instead of an *oblate* spheroid. * * The measurements of small arcs of the meridian in other countries have presented similar instances."*

A number of French Academicians who measured above three degrees of the meridian in Peru, gave as the result of their labours the first degree of the meridian from the equator as 56,653 toises; whilst another company of Academicians, who proceeded to Bothnia in Lapland, gave as the result of their calculation 57,422 toises for the length of a degree cutting the polar circle. But a more recent measurement made by the Swedish Astronomers in Bothnia shows the French to have been incorrect, having given the degree there 196 toises more than the true length. Other observations have been made, but as no two sets of experiments agree in result, it would be very unsatisfactory to conclude from them that the Earth is an oblate spheroid.

Returning to the pendulum, it will be found to be equally unsatisfactory as a proof of this peculiar rotundity of the Earth. It is argued that as the length of a seconds pendulum at the equator is 39,027 inches, and 39,197 inches at the north pole, that the Earth must be a globe, having a less diameter through its axis than through its equator. But this proceeds upon the *assumption* that the Earth *is* a globe having a "centre of attraction of gravitation," towards which all bodies gravitate or fall; and as the pendulum is a felling body under certain restraint, the fect that it oscillates or fells more rapidly at the north than it does at the equator, is a proof that the north is nearer to the centre of attraction, or the centre of the Earth, than is the equatorial region ; and, of course, if nearer, the radius must be shorter ; and therefore the "Earth is a spheroid flattened at the poles." This is very ingenious and very plausible, but, unfortunately for its character as an argument, the essential evidence is wanting that the Earth is a globe at all ! whether oblate or oblong, or truly spherical, are questions logically misplaced. It should also be first proved that *no other* cause could operate besides greater proximity to the centre of gravity, to produce the variable oscillations of a pendulum. This not being attempted, the whole subject must be condemned as logically insufficient, irregular, and worthless for its intended purpose. Many philosophers have ascribed the alterations in the oscillations of a pendulum to the diminished temperature of the northern centre. That the heat gradually and almost uniformly diminishes on passing from the equator to the north is well ascertained. "The mean annual temperature of the whole Earth at the level of the sea is 50° Fah. For different latitudes it is as under : –

			Degrees.			Inches.
Latitude (Equator)		0 ...	84.2	Length of	Pendulum	39,027
"	"	10 ...	... 82·6	"	"	"
"	"	20 ...	... 78·1	"	"	"
"	"	30 ...	... 71·1	"	"	"
"	"	40 ...	... 62·6	"	"	"
"	(London)	50 ...	... 53·6	"	"	39,139
"	"	60 ...	... 45·0	"	"	"
"	"	70 ...	... 38·1	"	"	"
"	"	80 ...	... 33·6	"	"	"
"	(Pole)	90 ...	... 00·0	"	"	39,197*"

"All the solid bodies with which we are surrounded are constantly undergoing changes of bulk corresponding to the variations of temperature. * * The expansion and contraction of metals by heat and cold form subjects of serious and careful attention to chronometer makers, as will appear by the following statements : – The length of the pendulum vibrating seconds, in vacuo, in the latitude of London (51° 31' 8" north), at the level of the sea, and at the temperature of 62°, has been ascertained with the greatest precision to be 39·13929 inches: now, as the metal of which it is composed is constantly subject to variation of temperature, it cannot but happen that its *length* is constantly

SECTION I. Introduction – Experiments proving the Earth to be a Plane

varying ; and when it is further stated that if the "bob" be let down 1-100th of an inch, the clock will lose 10 seconds in 24 hours ; that the elongation of 1-1000th of an inch will cause it to lose one second per day ; and that a change of temperature equal to 30° Fah. will alter its length 1-5000th part and occasion an error in the rate of going of 8 seconds per day, it will appear evident that some plan must be devised for obviating so serious an inconvenience."*

From these data it is readily seen that the variations in the rate of a pendulum as it is carried from the equator towards the north are sufficiently explained, without supposing that they arise from a peculiar spheroidal form of the Earth.

Others have attributed the variable motions of the pendulum to increased density of the air on going northwards. That the condition of the air must have some influence in this respect will be seen from the following extract from experiments on pendulums by Dr. Derham, recorded in numbers 294 and 480 of the *Philosophical Transactions* : – "The arches of vibration *in vacuo* were larger than in the open air, or in the receiver before it was exhausted ; the enlargement or diminution of the arches of vibration were *constantly proportional* to the *quantity of air,* or rarity, or density of it, which was left in the receiver of the air-pump. And as the *vibrations* were *longer* or *shorter*, *so* the *times* were accordingly, viz., two seconds in an hour when the vibrations were longest, and less and less as the air was re-admitted, and the vibrations shortened."

Thus there are two distinct and tangible causes which necessarily operate to produce the variable oscillations of a pendulum, without supposing any distortion in the supposed rotundity of the Earth. First, if the pendulum vibrates in the air, which is colder and therefore denser in the north chan at the equator, it must be more or less resisted in its passage through it ; and, secondly, if it vibrates *in vacuo*, the temperature being less, the length must be less, the arcs of vibration less, and the velocity greater. In going towards the equator, the temperature increases, the length becomes greater, the arcs increase, and the times of vibration diminish..

Another argument for the globular form of the Earth is the following : – The degrees of longitude radiating from the north pole gradually increase in extent as they approach the equator ; beyond which they again converge towards the south. To this it is replied that no actual measurement of a degree of longitude has ever been made south of the equator ! If it be said that mariners have sailed round the world in the southern region and have *computed* the length of the degrees, it is again replied that such evidence is unfavourable to the doctrine of rotundity. It will be seen from the following table of what the degrees of longitude would be if the earth were a globe of 25,000 miles circumference, and comparing these with the results of practical navigation, that the diminution of degrees of longitude beyond the equator is purely imaginary.

Latitudes at different longitudes : –

Latitude 1 = 59·99 nautical miles.
        10 = 59·09   "   "
        20 = 56·38   "   "
        30 = 51·96   "   "
        34 = 49·74 (Cape Town)
        40 = 45·96   "   "
        45 = 42·45 (Port Jackson, Sydney)
        50 = 38·57   "   "
        56 = 33·55 (Cape Horn)
        60 = 30·00   "   "
Latitude 65 = 25·36 nautical miles.
        70 = 20·52   "   "
        75 = 15·53   "   "
        80 = 10·42   "   "
        85 = 5·53   "   "
        86 = 4·19   "   "
        87 = 3·14   "   "
        88 = 2·09   "   "
        89 = 1·05   "   "
        90 = 0·00   "   "

According to the above table (which is copied from a large Mercator's chart in the library of the Mechanics' Institute, Royal Hill, Greenwich), the distance round the Earth at the Antarctic circle would only be about 9,000 miles. But practical navigators give the distance from the Cape of Good Hope to Port Jackson as 8,000 miles; from Port Jackson to Cape Horn as 8,000 miles ; and from Cape Horn to the Cape of Good Hope, 6,000 miles, making together 22,000 miles. The average longitude of these places is 45°, at which parallel the circuit of the Earth, if it be a globe, should only be 14,282 miles. Here, then, is an error between the theory of rotundity and practical sailing of 7,718 miles. But there are several statements made by Sir James Clarke Ross which tend to make the disparity even greater : at page 236, vol. 2, of "South Sea Voyages," it is said "From near Cape Horn to Port Philip (in Melbourne, Australia) the distance is 9,000 miles." These two places are 143 degrees of longitude from each other. Therefore the whole extent of the Earth's circumference is a mere arithmetical question. If 143 degrees make 9,000 miles, what will be the distance made by the whole 360 degrees into which the surface is divided ? The answer is, 22,657 miles ; or, 8357 miles more than the theory of rotundity would permit It must be borne in mind, however, that the above distances are nautical measure, which, reduced to statute miles, gives the actual distance round the Southern region at a given latitude as 26,433 statute miles ; or nearly 1,500 miles more than the largest circumference ever assigned to the Earth at the equator.

SECTION I. Introduction – Experiments proving the Earth to be a Plane

But actual measurement of a degree of longitude in Australia or some other land far south of the equator can alone place this matter beyond dispute. The problem to be solved might be given as the following : – A degree of longitude in England at the latitude of 50° N. is 38·57 nautical or 45 statute miles ; at the latitude of Port Jackson in Australia, which is 45° S., a degree of longitude, if the Earth is a globe, should be 42 45 nautical or 49·52 statute miles But if the Earth is a plane, and the distances above referred to as given by nautical men are correct, a degree of longitude on the parallel of Port Jackson will be 69·44 statute miles, being a difference of 19·92 or nearly 20 statute miles. In other words, a degree of longitude along the southern part of Australia ought to be, *if the Earth is a plane,* nearly 20 miles greater than a degree of longitude on the southern coast of England. This is the point which has yet to be settled. The day is surely not far distant when the scientific world will demand that the question be decided by proper geodetical operations ! And this not altogether for the sake of determining the true figure of the Earth, but also for the purpose of ascertaining, if possible, the cause of the many anomalies observed in navigating the southern region. These anomalies have led to the loss of many vessels and the sacrifice of a fearful amount of life and property. "In the southern hemisphere, navigators to India have often fancied themselves east of the Cape when still West, and have been driven ashore on the African coast, which according to their reckoning lay behind them. This misfortune happened to a fine frigate, the "Challenger," in 1845."* "Assuredly there are many shipwrecks from alleged errors in reckoning which *may* arise from a somewhat false idea of the general form and measurement of the Earth's surface. Such a subject, therefore, ought to be candidly and boldly discussed."†

It is commonly believed that surveyors when laying out railways and canals, are obliged to allow 8 inches per mile for the Earth's curvature ; and that if this were not done in the latter case the water would not be stationary, but would flow on until at the end of one mile in each direction, although the canal should have the same depth throughout, the surface would stand 8 inches higher in the middle than at the ends. In other words, that the bottom of a canal in which the allowance of 8 inches per mile had not been made, would be a chord to the surface of the contained water, which would be an arc of a circle. To this it is replied, that both in regard to railways and canals, wherever an allowance has been attempted the work has not been satisfactory ; and so irregular were the results in the earlier days of railway, canal, and other surveying, that the most eminent engineers abandoned the practice of the old "forward levelling" and allowing for convexity; and adopted what is now called the "double sight" or "back-and-fore sight" method. It was considered that whether the surface were convex or horizontal, or whether the convexity were more or less than the supposed degree, would be of no consequence in practice if the spirit level or theodolite were employed to read both backwards and forwards ; for whatever degree of convexity existed, one "sight" would compensate for the other; and if the surface were horizontal, the same mode of levelling would apply. So important did the ordnance department of the Government consider this matter, that it was deemed necessary to make the abandonment of all ideas of rotundity compulsory, and in a standing order (No. 6) of the House of Lords as to the preparation of sections for railways, &c., the following language is used, "That the section be drawn to the same *horizontal* scale as the plan ; and to a vertical scale of not less than one inch to every one hundred feet ; and shall show the surface of the ground marked on the plan, the intended level of the proposed work, the height of every embankment, and the depth of every cutting ; and a *datum* horizontal line, which shall be *the same throughout the whole length of the work,* or any branch thereof respectively ; and shall be referred to some fixed point stated in writing on the section, near some portion of such work ; and in the case of a canal, cut, navigation, turnpike, or other carriage road, or railway, near either of the termini" No. 44 of the standing orders of the House of Commons is similar to the above order (No. 6) of the House of Lords.

Thus it is evident that the doctrine of the Earth's rotundity cannot be mixed up with the practical operations of civil engineers and surveyors, and to prevent the waste of time and the destruction of property which necessarily followed the doings of some who were determined to involve the convexity of the Earth's surface in their calculations, the very Government of the country has been obliged to interfere ! Every survey of this and other countries, whether ordnance or otherwise, is now carried out in connection with a horizontal datum, and therefore, as no other method proves satisfactory, it is virtually an admission by all the most practical scientific men of the day that the Earth *cannot be other than a plane !*

An argument for the Earth's convexity is thought by many to be found in the following facts: – "Fluid or semi-fluid substances in a state of motion invariably assume the globular form, as rain, hail, dew, mercury, and melted lead, which, poured from a great height becomes divided into spherical masses, as in the manufacture of small shot, &c." "There is abundant evidence from geology that the Earth has been a fluid or semi-fluid mass, and it could not, therefore, continue in a state of motion through space without becoming spherical." Without denying that the Earth has been, at some former period, in a pulpy or semi-fluid state, it is requisite to prove beyond all doubt that it has a motion upon axes and through space, or the conclusion that it is therefore spherical is premature and illogical. It will be shown in a subsequent part of this work, that such axial and orbital motion does not exist, and therefore any argument founded upon and including it as a fact is necessarily fallacious. In addition to this, it may be remarked that the tendency in falling fluids to become globular is owing to what has been called "attraction of cohesion" (not "attraction of gravitation"), which is very limited in its operation. It is confined to small quantities of matter. If, in the manufacture of small shot, the melted metal is allowed to fall in masses of several ounces or pounds, instead of being

SECTION I. Introduction – Experiments proving the Earth to be a Plane

divided into particles weighing only a few grains; it will never take a spherical form, and shot of an inch in diameter could not be made by this process. Bullets of even half-an-inch diameter can only be made by casting the metal into spherical moulds. In tropical countries, the rain instead of falling in drops or small globules, often comes down in large irregular masses, which have no approximation whatever to sphericity. So that it is manifestly unjust to affirm of large masses of matter like the Earth that which only belongs to minute portions or a few grains in weight. The whole matter taken together entirely fails as an argument for the Earth's rotundity.

Those who hold that the Earth is a globe will often affirm, with visible enthusiasm, that in an eclipse of the Moon there is proof positive of rotundity. That the shadow of the Earth upon the Moon is always round ; and that nothing but a globe could, in all positions, cast a circular shadow. Here again the essential requirements of an argument are wanting. It is *not proved* that the Moon is eclipsed *by a shadow*. It is *not proved* that the *Earth moves* in an orbit, and therefore takes *different positions:* It is *not proved* that the Moon receives her light from the Sun, and that therefore her surface is darkened by the Earth intercepting the Sun's light. It will be shown in the proper place that the Earth has no motion in space or on axes ; that it is not a shadow which eclipses the Moon ; that the Moon is not a reflector of the Sun's light, but is *self-luminous ;* and therefore could not possibly be obscured by *a shadow* from any object whatever. The subject is only introduced here because it forms one of the category of supposed evidences of the Earth's rotundity. But to call that an argument where every necessary proposition is assumed, is to stultify both the judgment and the reasoning powers !

Many place great reliance upon what is called the "spherical excess" observed in levelling, as a proof of the Earth's rotundity. In Castle's Treatise on Levelling it is stated that "the angles taken between any three points on the surface of the Earth by the theodolite, are, strictly speaking, spherical angles, and their sum must exceed 180 degrees ; and the lines bounding them are not the chords as they should be, but the tangents to the Earth. This excess is inappreciable in common cases, but in the larger triangles it becomes necessary to allow for it, and to diminish each of the angles of the observed triangle by one-third of the spherical excess. To calculate this excess, divide the area of the triangle in feet by the radius of the Earth in seconds and the quotient is the excess."

The following observation as made by surveyors, also bears upon the subject : – If a spirit-level or theodolite be "levelled," and a given point be read upon a graduated staff at the distance of about or more than 100 chains, this point will have an altitude slightly in excess of the altitude of the cross-hair of the theodolite ; and if the theodolite be removed to the position of the graduated staff and again levelled, and a backward sight taken to the distance of 100 chains, another excess of altitude will be observed ; and this excess will go on increasing as often as the experiment or backward and forward observation is repeated. From this it is argued that the line of sight from the spirit-level or theodolite is a tangent, and that the surface of the Earth is therefore spherical.

Of a similar character is the following observation : – If a theodolite or spirit-level be placed upon the sea-shore, and "levelled," and directed towards the sea, the line of the horizon will be observed to be a given amount below the cross-hair of the instrument, to which a certain dip, or inclination from the level will have to be given to bring the cross-hair and the sea horizon together. It is concluded that as the sea horizon is always observed to be below the cross-hair of the "levelled" theodolite, the line of sight is a tangent, the surface of the water convex, and therefore the Earth is a globe.

The conclusion derived from the last three observations is exceedingly plausible, and would completely satisfy the minds of scientific men as to the Earth's sphericity if a perfect explanation could not be given. The whole matter has been specially and carefully examined ; and one very simple experiment will show that the effects observed do not arise from rotundity in the Earth's surface, but from a certain peculiarity in the instruments employed. Take a convex lens or a magnifying glass and hold it over a straight line drawn across a sheet of paper. If the glass be so held that a part of the straight line can be seen *through* it, and another part seen *outside* it, a difference in the *direction* of the line will be observed, as shown in the diagram Figure 21. Let A B C represent a straight lina If a

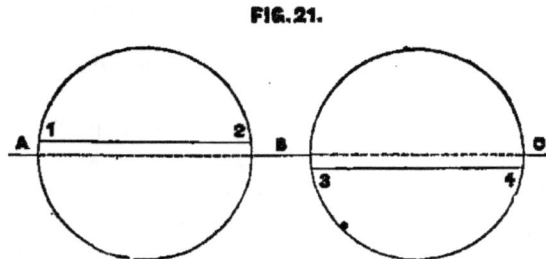

FIG. 21.

lens is now held an inch, or more, according to its focal length, over the part of the line A B, and the slightest amount out of its centre, that part of the line A B which passes under the lens will be seen in the direction of the figures 1.2 ; but if the lens be now moved a little out of its central position in the opposite direction, the line B C will be observed at 3.4, or below B C. A lens is a magnifying glass because it *dilates* or spreads out from its centre the objects observed through it Therefore whatever is magnified by it is seen a little out of its axis or centre. This is again necessitated by the fact that the axis or actual centre is always occupied by the cross-hair. Thus the line-of-sight in the theodolite or spirit-level not being axial or absolutely central, reads upon a

SECTION I. Introduction – Experiments proving the Earth to be a Plane

graduated staff a position which is necessarily slightly divergent from the axis of vision ; and this is the source of that "spherical excess" which has so long been considered by surveyors as an important proof of the Earth's rotundity. In this instance, as, indeed, in all the others given as evidence that the Earth is a globe, the premises do not fully warrant the conclusion – which is premature, – drawn before the whole subject is fairly examined ; and when other causes are amply sufficient to explain the effects observed.

Notes

* "An Account of Sir Isaac Newton's Discoveries." By Professor Maclaurin, M.A., F.R.S., of the Chair of Mathematics in the University of Edinburgh.
* "Liebig's Agricultural Chemistry," p. 39.
* "Wonders of Science," by Mayhew, p. 357.
* Encyclopædia of Geography, by Hugh Murray and several Professors in the University of Edinburgh.
* "Million of Facts," by Sir Richard Phillips, p. 475.
* "Noad's Lectures on Chemistry," p 41.
* "Tour through Creation," by the Rev. Thomas Milner, M.A.
† "The Builder," Sept. 20, 1862, in a "review" of a recently-published work on Astronomy.

SECTION 2

THE EARTH NO AXIAL OR ORBITAL MOTION.

IF a ball be allowed to drop from the mast-head of a ship *at rest*, it will strike the deck at the foot of the mast. If the same experiment be tried with a ship *in motion*, the same result will be observed. Because, in the latter case, the ball is acted upon simultaneously by two forces at right angles to each other – one, the momentum given to it by the moving ship in the direction of its own motion, and the other the force of gravity, the direction of which is square to that of the momentum. The ball being acted upon by the two forces together will not go in the direction of either, but will take a diagonal course, as shown in the following diagram, Figure 22.

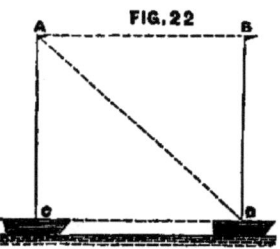

The ball passing from A to C by the force of gravity, and having at the moment of its liberation received a momentum from the ship in the direction A B, will by the conjoint action of the two forces, take the direction A D, falling at D, just as it would have fallen at C had the vessel remained at rest. In this way, it is contended by those who hold that the Earth is a moving sphere, a ball allowed to fall from the mouth of a deep mine reaches the bottom in an apparently vertical direction, the same as it would if the Earth were motionless. So far, there need be no discussion – the explanation is granted. But now let the experiment be modified in the following way: – Let the ball be thrown *upwards from* the mast-head of a moving vessel; it will partake as before of two modified in the following way : let the ball be thrown *upwards* from the mast-head of a moving vessel ; it will partake as before of two motions, the upward and the horizontal, and will take a diagonal course upwards and with the vessel until the two forces expend themselves, when it will begin to fall by the force of gravity only, and drop into the water far behind the ship, which is still moving horizontally. Diagram Figure 23 will illustrate this effect.

SECTION II. The Earth no Axial or Orbital Motion

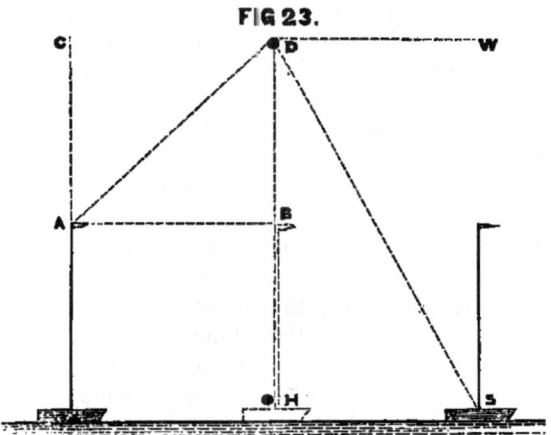

FIG 23.

The ball being thrown upwards in the direction A C, and the vessel moving from A to B, will cause it to pass in the direction A D, arriving at D when the vessel reaches B ; the two forces having expended themselves when the ball arrives at D, it will begin to descend by the force of gravity in the direction D B H, but during its fall the vessel will have reached the position S, so that the ball will drop far behind it at the point H. To bring the ball from D to S *two forces* would be required, as D H and D W ; but as D W does not exist, the force of gravity operates *alone,* and the ball necessarily falls behind the vessel at a distance proportionate to the altitude attained at D, and the time occupied in falling from D to H.

The same result will be observed on throwing a ball directly upwards from a railway carriage when in rapid motion, as shown in the following Figure 24. While the carriage or tender passes

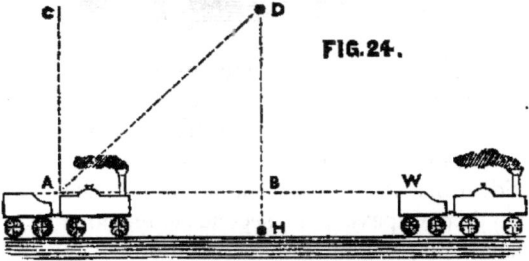

FIG. 24.

from A to B, the ball thrown from A to C will reach the position D, but while the ball then comes down by the force of gravity, *operating alone*, to the point H, the carriage will have advanced to W, so that the ball will always drop more or less behind the carriage, according to the force first given to it in the direction

- 37 -

A C and the time occupied in ascending to D, and thence descending to H. It is therefore demanded that if the Earth had a motion upon axes from west to east, and a ball, instead of being dropped down a mine or allowed to fall from the mast head of a ship, be *shot upwards* into the air ; from the moment of its beginning to descend the surface of the Earth would turn from under its direction, and it would fall behind or to the west of its line of descent. On making the experiment *no such effect is observed*, and therefore the conclusion is unavoidable, that the Earth does not move upon axes !

The following experiment has been tried, with the object of obtaining definite results. If the Earth is a globe, having a circumference of 25,000 miles at the equator, the circumference at the latitude of London (51°) will be about 16,000 statute miles ; so that the motion of the Earth's surface, if 25,000 miles in 24 hours at the equator, in England would be more than 700 feet per second. An air-gun was firmly fixed to a strong post, as shown at A in Figure 25, and carefully adjusted by a plumb-line, so that it was perfectly vertical On discharging the gun, the

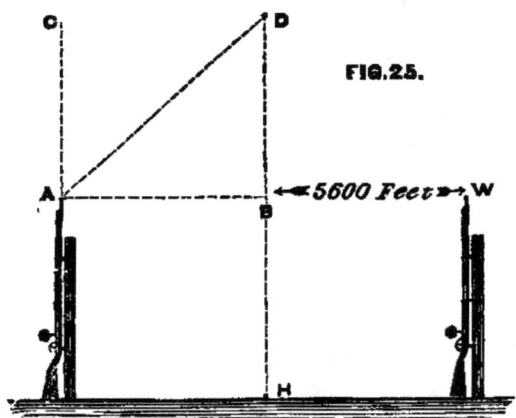

ball ascended in the direction A C, and invariably (during several trials) descended within a few inches of the gun at A ; twice it fell back upon the very mouth of the barrel The average time that the ball was in the atmosphere was 16 seconds ; and, as half the time would be required for the ascent and half for the descent, it is evident that if the Earth had a motion once round its axis in 24 hours, the ball would have passed in 8 seconds to the point D, while the air-gun would have reached the position B H. The ball then commencing its descent, requiring also 8 seconds, would in that time have feilen to *the point* H, while the Earth and the gun would have advanced as far as W. The time occupied being 8 seconds, and the Earth's velocity being 700 feet per second, the progress of the Earth and the air-gun to W, in advance of the ball at H, would be 5,600 feet ! In other words, in these experiments, the ball, which always fell back to the place

SECTION II. The Earth no Axial or Orbital Motion

of its detachment, should have fallen 5,600 feet, or considerably more than one statute mile to the west of the air-gun ! Proving beyond all doubt that the supposed axial motion of the Earth does not exist !

The same experiment ought to suffice as evidence against the assumed motion of the Earth in an orbit ; for it is difficult, if not impossible, to understand how the behaviour of the ball thrown from a vertical air-gun should be other in relation to the Earth's forward motion in space than it is in regard to its motion upon axes. Besides, if it is proved *not* to move upon axes, the assumption that it moves in an orbit round the Sun is useless for theoretical purposes, and there is no necessity for either denying or in any way giving it farther consideration. But that no point may be taken without direct evidence, let the following experiment be tried : – Take two carefully-bored iron tubes, about two yards in length, and place them, one yard asunder, on the opposite sides of a wooden frame, or a solid block of wood or masonry ; so adjust them that their axes of vision shall be perfectly parallel to each other, and direct them to the plane of some notable fixed star, a few seconds previous to its meridian time. Let an observer be stationed at each tube ; and the moment the star appears in the first tube, let a knock or other signal be given, to be repeated by the observer at the second tube when he first sees the star. A distinct period of time will elapse between the signals given, showing that the same star is not visible at the same moment by two lines of sight parallel to each other and only one yard asunder. A slight inclination of the second tube towards the first would be required for the star to be seen at the same moment. If now the tubes be left in their position for six months, the same star will be visible at the same meridian time, without the slightest alteration being required in the direction of the tubes. From which result it is concluded that if the Earth had moved *a single yard* in an orbit through space there would at least be the difference of time indicated by the signals, and the slight inclination of the tube which the difference in position of one yard required. But as no such difference in the direction of the tube is required, the conclusion is unavoidable that in six months a given *meridian upon* the Earth has not moved a single yard, and that therefore the Earth has not the slightest degree of orbital motion – or motion at right angles to the meridian of a given star ! It will be useless to say in explanation that the stars are so infinitely distant that a difference in the angle of inclination of the tube in six months could not be expected, as it will be proved in a subsequent section that *all* the stars are within a few thousand miles from the Earth's surface!

SECTION 3.

THE TRUE DISTANCE OF THE SUN AND STARS.

AS it is now demonstrated that the Earth is a plane, the distance of the Sun and Stars may readily be measured by plane trigonometry. The base line in any operation being horizontal and always a carefully measured one, the process becomes exceedingly simple. Let the altitude of the Sun be taken on a given day at 12 o'clock at the high-water mark on the sea shore at Brighton, in Sussex ; and at the same hour at the high-water mark of the River Thames, near London Bridge; the difference in the Sun's altitude taken simultaneously from two stations upon the same meridian, and the distance between the stations, or the length of the base line ascertained, are all the elements required for calculating the exact distance of the Sun from London or Brighton ; but as this distance is the hypothenuse of a triangle, whose base is the Earth's surface, and vertical side the zenith distance of the Sun, it follows that the distance of the Sun from that part of Earth to which it is vertical is less than the distance from London. In the Diagram, Figure 26, let L B represent the base line from London to Brighton, a

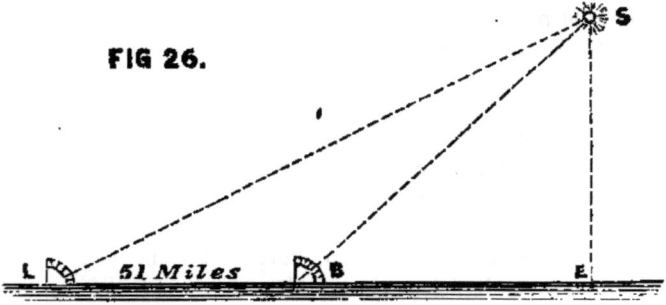

distance of 51 statute miles. The altitude at L and at B taken at the same moment of time will give the distance L S or B S. The angle of altitude at L or B, with the length of L S or B S, will then give the vertical distance of the Sun S from E, or the place which is immediately underneath it. This distance will be thus found to be considerably less than 4,000 miles.

The following are the particulars of an observation made, a few years age, by the officers engaged in the Ordnance survey. Altitude of the Sun at London 55° 13'; altitude taken at the same time, on the grounds of a public school, at Ackworth, in Yorkshire, *53° 2' ;* the distance between the two places in a direct line, as measured by triangulation, is 151 statute miles. From these elements the true distance of the Sun may be readily computed ; and proved to be under 4,000 miles !

SECTION III. The true distance of the Sun and Stars

Since the above was written, an officer of the Royal Engineers, in the head-quarters of the Ordnance Survey, at Southampton, has furnished the following elements of observations recently made : –

      Southern Station, Sun's altitude, 45°
      Northern ditto,   "   "   38°
Distance between the two stations, 800 statute miles.

The calculation made from these elements gives the same result, viz., that the actual distance of the Sun from the Earth is less than 4,000 miles.

The same method of measuring distances applies equally to the Stars ; and it is easy to demonstrate, beyond the possibility of doubt, so long as assumed premises are excluded, that all the visible objects in the firmament are contained within the distance of 6,000 miles !

From these demonstrable distances it follows unavoidably that the *magnitude* of the Sun, Moon, Stars, &c., is very small – much smaller than the Earth from which they are measured ; and to which therefore they cannot possibly be other than secondary, and subservient

SECTION 4.

THE SUN MOVES IN A CIRCLE OVER THE EARTH, CONCENTRIC WITH THE NORTH POLE.

As the Earth has been shown to be fixed, the motion of the Sun is a visible reality ; and if it be observed from any northern latitude, and for any period before and after the time of southing, or passing the meridian, it will be seen to describe an arc of a circle ; an object moving in an arc cannot return to the centre of such arc without having completed a circle. This the Sun does visibly and daily. To place the matter beyond doubt, the observation of the Arctic navigators may be referred to. Captain Parry, and several of his officers, on ascending high land in the vicinity of the north pole, repeatedly saw, for 24 hours together, the sun describing a circle upon the southern horizon.

SECTION 5.

THE DIAMETER OF THE SUN'S PATH IS CONSTANTLY CHANGING – DIMINISHING FROM DECEMBER 21st TO JUNE 15th, AND ENLARGING FROM JUNE TO DECEMBER

THIS is a matter of absolute certainty, proved by what is called, in technical language, the northern and southern declination, which is simply saying that the Sun's path is nearest the north pole in summer, and farthest away from it in winter. This difference in position gives rise to the difference of altitude, as observed at various periods of the year, and which is shewn in the following table, given in "The Illustrated London Almanack," for 1848, by Mr. Glaisher, of the Royal Observatory, Greenwich.

"Sun's altitude at the time of Southing, or being on the meridian : –

Date		Sun's altitude.	Time of Southing. M. S.	(Common clock, or London mean time.)
June 15	... ...	62	0 4	before noon.
" 30	... ...	61⅔°	3 18	afternoon,
July 15	... ...	59⅔°	5 38	"
" 31	... ...	56½°	6 4	"
Aug. 15	... ...	52½°	0 11	"
" 31	... ...	47°	0 5	"
Sep. 15	... ...	38⅔°	4 58	before noon
" 30	... ...	35½°	10 6	"
Oct. 31	... ...	24°	16 14	"
Nov. 30	... ...	17°	10 58	"
Dec. 21	... ...	12°	0 27	"
" 31	... ...	15°	3 29	afternoon.
Jan. 1	... ...	15½°	3 36	"
" 15	... ...	17°	9 33	"
" 31	... ...	21°	13 41	"
Feb. 15	... ...	25°	14 28	"
" 29	... ...	30½°	12 43	"
March 15	{On the equator at 6 a.m.}	36°	9 2	"
		38½°	0 0	"
" 21	... ...	42½°	4 10	before noon.
April 15	... ...	48°	0 8	"
" 30	... ...	53°	2 58	"
May 15	... ...	57°	3 54	"
" 31	... ...	60°	2 37	"

In the following diagram (Fig. 27) A A A represent the Sun's daily path on December 21st, and B B B the same on June 15th. N the North Pole, S the Sun, E Great Britain. The figures 1 2 3 the Arctic Circle, and 4 5 6 the extent of sunlight The arrows show the direction of the Sun's motion.

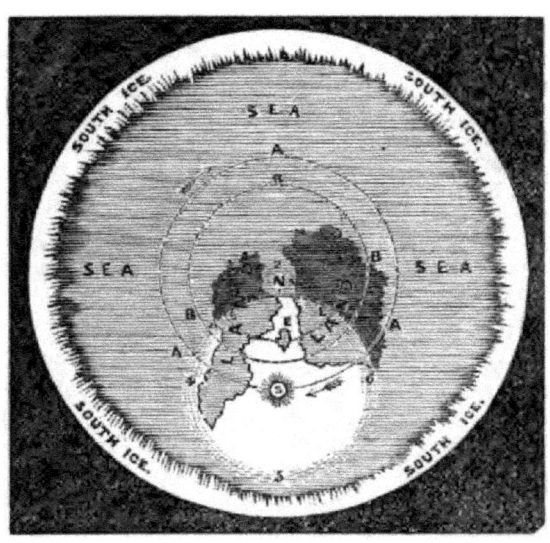

SECTION 6.

CAUSE OF DAY AND NIGHT, SEASONS, &C.

The Sun S describes the circle A A A on the 21st December once in 24 hours ; hence in that period day and night occur to every part of the Earth, except within the Arctic circle. The light of the Sun gradually diminishing from S, to the Arctic circle 1 2 3, where it becomes twilight, does so according to the well-known law of radiation, equally in all directions – hence, the circle 4 5 6 represents the whole extent of the Sun's light at any given time. The arc 4 E is the advancing or morning twilight, and 6 E the receding or evening twilight ; to every place underneath a line drawn across the circle through S to N it is noonday. It will now be easily understood that as the Sun S moves in the direction of the arrows or from right to left, and completes the circle A A A in 24 hours, it will produce in that period morning, noon, evening, and night to all parts of the Earth in succession. On referring to the diagram, it will be seen that to England, E, the length of the day at this time of the year is the *shortest*, the amount of light being represented by the arc E E E ; and also that the northern centre N remains in darkness during the whole daily revolution of the Sun, the light of which terminates at the Arctic circle 1 2 3. Thus, morning, noon, evening, midnight, the *shortest* days, or the Winter season, and the constant or six months' darkness at the pole are all a part of one general phenomenon. As the Sun's path begins now to diminish every day until in six months, or on the 15th of June, it describes the circle B B B, it is evident that the same extent of sunlight will reach over or beyond the pole N, as shown in the following diagram (Fig. 28), when morning, noon, evening, and night will again occur as before ; but the amount of light passing over England, represented by the arc E E E, is now much larger than when the Sun was upon the circle A A A, and represents the *longest* days, or the *Summer* season, and the constant, or six months' light at the pole. Thus, day and night, long and short days, Winter and Summer, the long periods of alternate light and darkness at the pole, arise simply from the Sun's position in relation to the north pole.

ZETETIC ASTRONOMY. EARTH NOT A GLOBE!

If the Earth is a globe, it is evident that Winter and Summer, and long and short days, will be of the same character and duration in corresponding latitudes, in the southern as in the northern hemisphere. But we find that in many respects there is a marked difference ; for instance, in New Zealand, where the latitude is about the same as in England, a remarkable difference exists in the length of day and night. In the Cook's Strait Almanack, for 1848, it is stated, "At Wellington, New Zealand, December 21, Sun rises 4h. 31m., and sets at 7L 29m., the day being 14 hours 58 minutes. June 21st, Sun rises at 7h. 29m., and sets at 4L 31m., the day being 9 hours and 2 minutes. In England the longest day is 16h. 34m., and the shortest day is 7h. 45m. Thus the *longest day* in New Zealand is 1 hour and 36 minutes *shorter* than the *longest day* in England ; and the s*hortest day* in New Zealand is 1 hour and 17 minutes *longer* than the shortest day in England."

In a recently published pamphlet, by W. Swainson, Esq., Attorney General, the following passage occurs : – "Compared with an English summer, that of Auckland is but little warmer, though much longer; but the nights in New Zealand are always cool and refreshing. . . . . The days are *one hour shorter* in the summer, and *one hour longer* in the winter than in England ! of *twilight* there is *little* or *none.*"

From a work, also recently published, on New Zealand, by Arthur S. Thompson, M.D., the following sentences are quoted : – "The summer mornings, even in the warmest parts of the colony are sufficiently fresh to exhilarate without chilling ; and the seasons glide imperceptibly into each other. The days are *an hour shorter* at *each end* of the day in summer, and an hour longer in winter than in England."

SECTION VI. Cause of Day and Night, Seasons, &c.

A letter from a correspondent in New Zealand, dated Nelson, September 15, 1857, contains the subjoined passages : – "Even in summer people here have no notion of going without fires in the evening ; but then, though the days are very warm and sunny, the nights are always cold For seven months last summer we had not one day that the Sun did not shine as brilliantly as it *does* in England in the finest day in June ; and though it has more power here, the heat is not nearly so oppressive. . . . But then there is not the twilight which you get in England Here it is light till about eight o'clock ; then, in a few minutes, it becomes too dark to see anything, and the change comes over in almost no time." "Twilight lasts but a short time in so low a latitude as 28 degrees, and no sooner does the Sun peep above the horizon, than all the gorgeous parade by which he is preceded is shaken off, and he comes in upon us in the most abrupt and unceremonious way imaginable."* These various peculiarities could *not* exist in the southern region if the Earth were spherical and moved upon axes, and in an orbit round the Sun. If the Sun is fixed, and the Earth revolves underneath it, the same phenomena should exist at the same distance on each side of the Equator. But such is not the case ! What can operate to cause the twilight in New Zealand to be so much more sudden than it is in England? The southern "hemisphere" cannot revolve more rapidly than the northern ! The distance round *a globe* would be the same at 50° south as at 60° north, and as the whole globe would revolve once in 24 hours, the surface at the two places would move underneath the Sun with the same velocity, and the light would approach in the morning and recede in the evening in exactly the same manner ; yet the *very contrary* is the fact ! The twilight in England in summer is slow and gradual, but in New Zealand it is rapid and abrupt ; a difference which is altogether incompatible with the doctrine of the Earth's rotundity. But, the Earth a plane, and it is a simple "matter of course." Let E, in Figure 28, represent England, and W New Zealand ; the radius N E and the consequent circle round N is much less than the radius N W and its consequent circle round the same point But as the larger circle, radius N W is passed over by the sunlight in the same time (24 hours) as the smaller circle, radius N E, the velocity is proportionately greater. The velocity is the space passed over multiplied by the time in passing, and as the space over New Zealand is much greater than the space over England, the velocity of the Sun-light must be much greater, and its morning and evening twilight necessarily more "abrupt and unceremonious and *therefore,* it might be said with strictly logical accuracy, the Earth is a Plane, and cannot possibly be a Globe !

Note

* Captain Basil Hall, R.N., F.R.S.

SECTION 7.

CAUSE OF "SUNRISE" AND "SUNSET."

ALTHOUGH the Sun is at all times above and parallel to the Earth's surface, he appears to ascend the firmament from morning until noon, and to descend and sink below the horizon at evening. This arises from a simple and everywhere visible law of perspective. A flock of birds, when passing over a flat or marshy country, always appears to descend as it recedes ; and if the flock is extensive, the first bird appears lower, or nearer to the horizon than the last. When a balloon sails from an observer without increasing or decreasing its altitude, it appears gradually to approach the horizon. The farthest light in a row of lamps appears the lowest, although each one has the same altitude. Bearing these phenomena in mind, it will easily be seen how the Sun, although always parallel to the surface of the Earth, must appear to ascend when approaching, and descend after leaving the meridian or noon-day position. Let the line A B, Fig. 29, represent a portion of the Earth's surface ; C D of the Sun's path and H H, the

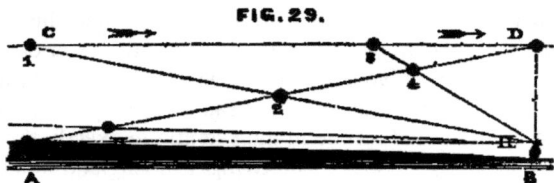

line of sight. The surface of the Earth, A B, will appear to ascend from B to H, forming the horizon. When the Sun is traversing the line C D, in the direction of the arrows, he will appear to emerge from the horizon H, and to gradually ascend the line H D. When in the position 1, he will *appear* to be at the point 2 ; and when at 3, the apparent position will be at 4 ; but when he arrives upon the meridian D, his apparent and actual, or noon-day position, will be the same. But now, from the point D, the Sun will appear to descend, as in Fig. 30, and when he

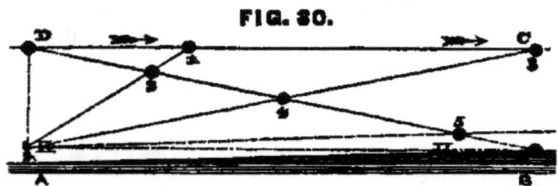

has passed from D to 1, he will appear at 2, and *when really at* 3 will appear at 4 ; and thus continuing his course in the direction D C, he will reach the horizon at H, and disappear or "set" to the observer at H A. Thus "Sunrise" and "Sunset" are phenomena dependent entirely upon the fact that horizontal lines parallel to each other appear to approach or converge in the distance, the surface of the Earth being horizontal, and the line-of-sight of the observer and the Sun's path being parallel with it, necessarily produce the observed phenomena.

SECTION 8.

CAUSE OF SUN APPEARING LARGER WHEN RISING AND SETTING THAN WHEN ON THE MERIDIAN.

IT is well known that when a light of any kind shines through a dense medium it will appear larger than when seen through a lighter medium. This will be more remarkable when the medium holds aqueous particles in solution, – as in a damp or foggy atmosphere the light of a gaslamp will seem greater at a given distance than it will under ordinary circumstances. In the diagram, Figure 30, it is evident that H D is less than H 1, H 3, or H 5. The latter (H 5) represents the greater amount of atmosphere which the Sun has to shine through when approaching the horizon; and as the air near the Earth is both more dense and more damp, or holds more watery particles in solution, the light of the Sun must be dilated or enlarged as well as modified in colour. But the enlarged appearance of the Sun when rising and setting is only an optical impression, as proved by actual measurement. "If the angle of the Sun or Moon be taken either with a tube or micrometer when they appear so large to the eye in the horizon, the measure is identical when they are in the meridian and appear to the eye and mind but half the size. The apparent distance of the horizon is three or four times greater than the zenith. Hence the mental mistake of horizontal size, for the angular dimensions are equal ; the first 5° is apparently to the eye equal to 10° or 15° at 50° or 60° of elevation ; and the first 15° fill a space to the eye equal to a third of the quadrant This is evidently owing to the ' habit of sight,' for with an accurate instrument the measure of 5° near the horizon is equal to 5° in the zenith"*

Note

* "Million of Facts," by Sir Richard Philips, p. 537.

SECTION 9.

CAUSE OF SOLAR AND LUNAR ECLIPSES.

AN Eclipse of the Sun is caused simply by the Moon passing before it, or between it and the observer on the Earth. Of this no question has been raised. But that an Eclipse of the Moon arises from a shadow of the Earth is in every respect unsatisfactory. The Earth has been proved to have no motion, either upon axes or in an orbit round the Sun, and therefore it could never come between the Sun and the Moon. The Earth is proved to be a Plane, always underneath the Sun and Moon, and therefore to speak of its intercepting the light of the Sun and thus casting its own shadow upon the Moon, is to say that which is impossible. Besides this, cases are on record of the Sun and Eclipsed Moon being above the horizon together. "The full Moon has sometimes been seen above the horizon before the Sun was set. A remarkable instance *of this kind was* observed at Paris on the 19th of July, 1750, when the Moon appeared visibly Eclipsed while the Sun was distinctly to be seen above the horizon."* "On the 20th of April, 1837, the Moon appeared to rise Eclipsed before the Sun had set The same phenomenon was observed on the 20th of September, 1717."† "In the lunar Eclipses of July 17, 1590 ; Nov. 3, 1648 ; June 16, 1666 ; and May 26, 1668, the Moon rose Eclipsed whilst the Sun was still apparently above the horizon. Those *horizontal* Eclipses were noticed as early as the time of Pliny."‡ The Moon's entire surface, or that portion presented to the Earth has also been distinctly seen during the whole time of a total Eclipse, a phenomenon utterly incompatible with the doctrine that the Earth's shadow is the cause of it. "The Moon has sometimes shown during a total Eclipe with an almost unaccountable distinctness. On Dec. 22, 1703, the Moon, when totally immersed in the Earth's shadow, was visible at Avignon by a ruddy light of such brilliancy that one might have imagined her body to be trasparent, and to be enlightened from behind ; and on March 19th, 1848, it is stated that so bright was the Moon's surface during its total immersion, that many persons could not be persuaded that it was eclipsed. Mr. Forster, of Bruges, states, in an account of that eclipse, that the light and dark places on the moon's surface could be almost as well made out as in an ordinary dull moonlight night

"Sometimes, in a total lunar eclipse, the moon will appear quite obscure in some parts of its surface, and in other parts will exhibit a high degree of illumination. * * * To a certain extent I witnessed some of these phenomena during the merely partial eclipse of February 7th, 1860. * * * I prepared, during the afternoon of February 6th for witnessing the eclipse, without any distinct expectation of seeing much worthy of note. I knew, however, that upwards of eight-tenths of the disc would be covered, and I was anxious to observe with

SECTION IX. Cause of Solar and Lunar Eclipses

what degree of distinctness the eclipsed portion could be viewed, partly as an interesting fact, and partly with a view of verifying or discovering the weak points of an engraving (in which I am concerned) of a lunar eclipse.

"After seeing the increasing darkness of the penumbra softly merging into the true shadow at the commencement of the eclipse (about 1 o'clock am., Greenwich time) I proceeded with *pencil and paper*, dimly lighted by a distant lamp, to note by name the different lunar mountains and plains (the so-called seas) over which the shadow passed * * * During the first hour and ten minutes I had seen nothing unexpected. * * * I had repeatedly written down my observations of the remarkable clearness with which the moon's eclipsed outline could be seen, both with the naked eye, and with the telescope ; at 1 hour 58 minutes, however, I suddenly noted the ruddy colour of a *portion* of the moon. I may as well give my notes in the original words, as copied next day in a more connected form : – 1h. 58m., Greenwich time. I am suddenly struck by the fact that the whole of the western seas of the moon are showing through the shadow with singular sharpness, and that the whole region where they lie has assumed a decidedly reddish tinge, attaining its greatest brightness at a sort of temporary polar region, having 'Endymion' about the position of its. imaginary pole I particularly notice that the 'Lake of Sleep' has disappeared in this brightness, instead of standing out in a darker shade : and I notice that this so-called polar region is not parallel with the rim of the shadow, but rather west of it – 2h. 15m. Some clouds, though very thin and transparent, now intervene. – 2h. 20m. The shy is now cleared, How extraordinary is the appearance of the Moon! *Reddish* is not the word to express it ; it is red – red hot ! I endeavour to think of various red objects with which to compare it, and nothing seems so like as a *red-hot penny* – a red-hot penny with a little *white*-hot piece at its lower edge, standing out against a dark-blue back ground; only it is evidently not a mere disc, but beautifully rounded by shading.

"Such is its appearance with the naked eye : with the telescope its surface varies more in tint than with the naked eye, and is not of quite so bright a red as when thus viewed. The redness continues to be most perceptible at a distance from the shadow's southern edge. and to be greatest about the region of 'Endymion.' The Hercynian mountains (north of Grimaldus) are, however, of rather a bright red, and Grimaldus shows well. Mare Crisium and the western seas are wonderfully distinct Not a trace to be seen of Aristarchus or Plato. – 2h. 27m. It is now nearly the middle of the eclipse. The red colour is very brilliant to the naked eye. * * * After this, I noticed a progressive change of tint in the Moon. – 2h. 50m. The Moon does not seem to the naked eye of so bright a red as before ; and again I am reminded by its tint of red-hot copper, or rather copper which has begun to cool. The whole of Grimaldi is now *uncovered.* Through the telescope I notice a decided grey shade at the lower part of the eclipsed portion, and the various small craters give it a stippled effect, like the old aqua-tint engravings. The upper part is reddish, but two graceful bluish curves, like horns, mark the form of the Hercynian mountains, and the bright region on the other limb of the Moon. These are visible also to the naked eye.

"At 3h. 5m. the redness had almost disappeared; a very few minutes afterwards, no trace of it remained, and ere long clouds came on. I watched the Moon, however, occasionally gaining a glimpse of its disc, till a quarter to four o'clock, when, for the last time on that occasion, I saw it faintly appearing through the clouds, nearly a full Moon again ; and then I took leave of it, feeling amply repaid for my vigil by the beautiful spectacle which I had seen."*

Mr Walkey, who observed the lunar eclipse of March 19th, 1848, near Collumpton, says – "The appearances were as usual till 20 minutes past 9 ; at that period, and for the space of the next hour, instead of an eclipse, or the shadow (umbra) of the Earth being the cause of the total obscurity of the Moon, the whole phase of that body became very quickly and most beautifully *illuminated;* and assumed the appearance of the glowing heat of fire from the furnace, rather tinged with a *deep red.* * * * The whole disc of the Moon being as *perfect with light* as if there had been *no eclipse whatever!* * * * The Moon positively gave *good light from its disc during the total eclipse!"*

In the astronomical portion of the "Illustrated London Almanack for 1864," by Mr. Glaisher, a beautiful tinted engraving is given representing the appearance of the Moon during the total eclipse of June 1, 1863, when all the light and dark places – the so-called mountains, seas, &c., were plainly visible. In the accompanying descriptive chapter, the following sentences occur: – "At the time of totality the Moon presented a soft woolly appearance, apparently more globular in form than when fully illuminated. Traces of the larger and brighter mountains were visible at the time of totality, and particularly the bright rays proceeding from Tycho, Kepler, and Aristarchus. * * * At first, when the obscured part was of small dimensions, it was of an iron grey tint, but as it approached totality, the reddish light became so apparent that it was remarked that the Moon 'seemed to be on fire and when the totality had commenced, it certainly looked like a fire smouldering in its ashes, and almost going out."

If then, the Sun and Moon have many times been seen above the horizon when the latter was eclipsed, how can it be said that the Earth's shadow was the cause of a lunar eclipse, when the Earth was not between or in a line with the Sun and Moon? And how can the Moon's non-luminous surface be distinctly visible and illuminated during the very totality of an eclipse, if all the light of the Sun is intercepted by the Earth?

Again, if the Moon is a sphere, which it is declared to be, how can its surface *reflect* the light of the Sun ? If her surface was a mass of polished silver, it could not reflect from more than a mere point ! Let a silvered glass ball or globe of considerable size be held before a lamp or fire of any magnitude, and it will be seen that instead of the whole surface reflecting light, there will be a very small portion only illuminated. But the Moon's *whole surface* is brilliantly illuminated ! a condition or effect utterly impossible if it be spherical. The surface *might* be

SECTION IX. Cause of Solar and Lunar Eclipses

illuminated from the Sun, or any other source if opaque, instead of polished, like an ordinary silvered mirror, but it could not shine intensely from every part, and brightly illuminate the objects before it, does so beautifully when full and in a clear firmament If the Earth *were admitted* to be globular, and to move, and to be capable of throwing a shadow by intercepting the light of the Sun, it would be impossible for a lunar eclipse to occur thereby, unless at the same time the Moon be proved to be non-luminous, and to shine only by reflection. But this is not proved ; it is only assumed as an essential part of a theory. The *contrary* is capable of proof, and proof beyond the power of doubt, viz., that the Moon is *self-luminous,* or shines with a light peculiar to herself, and therefore independently of the Sun. A reflector necessarily gives off what it receives. If a mass of red-hot metal be placed before a plane or concave surface, *heat* will be reflected. If snow or ice be similarly placed, *cold* will be reflected. If light, ordinary or coloured, be presented, the *same* will be reflected. If sound of a given pitch be produced, the same pitch will be reflected. If the note A be sounded upon a musical instrument, a reflector would not return the note B or C, but the *same note*, altered only in degree or intensity, hut not in "pitch." A reflector receiving a red light would rot return a blue or yellow light. A reflector collecting the cold from a mass of ice, would not throw off heat ; nor the contrary. *Nor* could the Moon, if a reflector, radiate or throw down upon the Earth any other light than such as she receives from the Sun. No difference could exist in the quality or character of the light, and it could differ in no respect but the quantity or intensity.

The light of the Sun and of the Moon are different in their general appearance – in the colour and action upon the eye.

The Sun's light is drying and preservative, or antiseptic. The Moon's light is damp and putrefactive.

The Sun's rays will put out a common fire ; the Moon's light will increase the combustion. The light of the Sun falling upon certain chemical substances, produces a change of colour, as in photographic and other processes. The light of the Moon fails to produce the same effect. Dr. Lardner, at page 121 of his excellent work, "The Museum of Science," says – "The most striking instance of the effect of certain rays of solar light in blackening a light-colored substance, is afforded by chloride of silver, which is a white substance, but which immediately becomes black when acted upon by the rays near the violet extremity of the spectrum. This substance, however, highly susceptible as it is of having its colour affected by light, is, nevertheless, found not to be changed in any sensible degree when exposed to Moon, even when that light is condensed by the most powerful burning lenses."

The Sun's light when concentrated by a number of mirrors, or a large burning lens, produces a focus which is entirely non-luminous, but in which the heat is so great that metallic and alkaline substances are quickly fused; earthy and mineral compounds almost immediately vitrified ; and all animal and vegetable structures in a few seconds burned up and destroyed. But the Moon's light so concentrated produces a brilliant focus, so luminous that it is difficult to look upon it ; and yet there is no increase of temperature! "If the most delicate thermometer be exposed to the full light of the Moon, shining with its greatest lustre, the mercury is not elevated a hair's breadth, neither would it be if exposed in the focus of her rays concentrated by the most powerful lenses. This has been proved by actual experiment."* "This question has been submitted to the test of direct experiment * * * The bulb of a thermometer sufficiently sensitive to render apparent a change of temperature amounting to the thousandth part of a degree, was placed in the focus of a concave reflector of vast dimensions, which, being directed to the Moon, the lunar rays were collected with great power upon it Not the slightest change, however, was produced in the thermometric column, proving that a concentration of rays sufficient to fuse gold, if they proceeded *from the Sun*, does not produce a change of temperature so great as the thousandth part of a degree, when they proceed *from the Moon."**

"The light of the Moon though concentrated by the most powerful burning glass, is incapable of raising the temperature of the most delicate thermometer. M. De La Hire collected the rays of the full Moon when on the meridian, by means of a burning glass thirty-five inches in diameter, and made them fall on the bulb of a delicate air-thermometer. *No effect was produced*, though the lunar rays by this glass were concentrated 300 times." "Professor Forbes concentrated the Moon's light by a lens thirty inches in diameter, its focal distance being about forty-one inches, and having a power of concentration exceeding 6,000 times. The image of the Moon which was only eighteen hours past full, and less than two hours from the meridian, was brilliantly thrown by this lens on the extremity of a commodious thermo-pile. Although the observations were made in the most unexceptional manner, and (supposing that half the rays were reflected, dispersed, and absorbed) though the light of the Moon was concentrated 3000 *times, not the slightest thermo-effect was produced!** In the "Lancet" (medical journal) for March 14th, 1856, particulars are given of several experiments, which proved that the Moon's rays when concentrated actually *reduced* the temperature upon a thermometer more than 8 degrees!

> "The cold chaste Moon, the Queen
> Of Heaven's bright Isles;
> Who makes all beautiful
> On which she smiles :
> That wandering shrine of soft
> Yet *icy flame*,
> Which ever is transformed
> Yet still the same ;
> And *warms not* but *illumes."*
>
> – SHELLEY.

SECTION IX. Cause of Solar and Lunar Eclipses

The "pale *cold* Moon" is an expression not only beautiful poetically but evidently true philosophically.

If, as we have now seen, the very nature of a reflector demands certain conditions and the Moon does not manifest these conditions, it must of necessity be concluded that the Moon is *not a reflector,* but a *self-luminous body.* If self-luminous her surface *could* not be darkened or eclipsed by a shadow of the Earth – supposing such were thrown upon it The luminosity instead of being diminished would be greater in proportion to the greater density or darkness of the shadow. As the light in a lantern shines most brightly in the darkest places, so would the Moon's self-luminous surface be most intense in the deepest part of the Earth's shadow. It is thus rendered undeniable that a Lunar Eclipse *does* not and *could* not arise from a shadow of the Earth ! As a *Solar* Eclipse occurs from the Moon passing over the Sun ; so from the evidence it is clear that a Lunar Eclipse *can only* arise from a similar cause – a body semi-transparent and well-defined passing before the Moon, or between her surface and the observer on the surface of the Earth. That such a body exists is admitted by several distinguished astronomers. In the report of the Council of the Royal Astronomical Society for June, 1850 it is stated, "We may well doubt whether that body which we call the Moon is the *only satellite* of the Earth." In the report of the Academy of Sciences for October 12, 1846, and again for August, 1847, the Director of one of the French Observatories gives a number of observations and calculations which have led him to conclude that "there is at least *one non-luminous body* of considerable magnitude which is attached as a *satellite to this Earth."*

Persons who are unacquainted with the methods of calculating Eclipses and other astronomical phenomena, are prone to look upon the correctness of these calculations as powerful arguments in favour of the doctrine of the Earth's rotundity and the Newtonian philosophy generally. But this is erroneous. Whatever theory is adopted, or if all theories are discarded, the same results may follow, because the necessary data may be tabulated and employed independently of all theory, or may be mixed up with any, even the most opposite doctrines, or kept distinct from every system, just as the operator may decide. The tables of the Moon's relative positions for almost any second of time are purely practical, the result of long continued observation, and may or may not be mixed up with hypothesis. In Smith's "Rise and progress of Astronomy," speaking of Ptolemy, who lived in the 2nd century of the Christian Era, it is said, "The (considered) defects of his system did not prevent him from calculating all the Eclipses that were to happen for 600 years to come." Professor Partington, at page 370 of his Lectures on Natural Philosophy, says, "The most ancient observations of which we are in possession, that are sufficiently accurate to be employed in astronomical calculations, are those made at Babylon about 719 before the Christian Era, of three Eclipses of the Moon. Ptolemy, who has transmitted them to us, employed them for determining the period of the Moon's mean motion; and therefore had probably none more ancient on which he could depend. The Chaldeans, however, must have made a long series of observations before they could discover their "Saros" or lunar period of 6,585⅓ days, or about 18 years ; at which time, as they had learnt, the place of the Moon, her *node* and *apogee* return nearly to the same situation with respect to the Earth and the Sun, and, of course, a series of nearly similar Eclipses occur."

Sir Richard Phillips, in his "Million of Facts," at page 388, says : – "The precision of astronomy arises, not from theories, but from prolonged observations, and the regularity of the motions, or the ascertained uniformity of their irregularities. Ephemerides of the planets* places, of Eclipses, &c., have been published for above 300 years, and were nearly as precise as at present"

"No particular theory is required to calculate Eclipses ; and the calculations may be made with equal accuracy *independent of every theory.*"*

Notes

* "Astronomy and Astronomical Instruments," p. 105, by Geo. G. Carey.
† "McCulloch's Geography," p. 85.
‡ "Illustrated London Almanack for 1864," the astronomical part in which is by James Glaisher, Esq., of the Greenwich Observatory.
* The Hon. Mrs. Ward, Trimleston House, near Dublin, in "Recreative Science," p. 281.
* "*Philosophical* Magazine," No. 220, for August, 1848.
* "All the Tear Round," by Dickens.
* Dr. Lardner's Museum of Science, p. 115.
* *Dr. Noad's* Lectures on Chemistry, p. 334.
* Referred to in Lardner's "Museum of Science," p. 159.
* Somerville's Physical Sciences, p. 46.

SECTION 10.

CAUSE OF TIDES.

THE doctrine of the Earth's rotundity being fallacious, all ideas of "centre of attraction of gravitation," "mutual attraction of Earth and Moon," &c., &c., must be given up ; and the cause of tides in the ocean must be sought for in another direction. It is certain that there is a constant pressure of the 'atmosphere upon the surface of the Earth and ocean. This is proved by ordinary barometrical observations, many Pneumatic experiments, and by the fact that during the most fearful storms at sea the surface only is disturbed ; at the depth of a hundred feet the water is always calm – except in the path of well-marked currents and local submarine phenomena. The following quotations gathered from casual reading fully corroborate this statement. "It is amazing how superficial is the most terrible tempest Divers assure us that in the greatest storms calm water is found at the depth of 90 feet."*

"This motion of the surface of the sea is not perceptible to a great depth. In the strongest gale it is supposed not to extend beyond 72 feet below the surface ; and at the depth of 90 feet the sea is perfectly still."*

"The people are under a great mistake who believe that the substance of the water moves to any considerable depth in a storm at sea. It is only the form or shadow which hurries along like a spirit, or like a thought over the countenance of the 'great deep,' at the rate of some forty miles an hour. Even when the 'Flying Dutchman' is abroad the great mass of water continues undisturbed and nearly motionless a few feet below the surface."†

"The unabraded appearance of the shells brought up from great depths, and the almost total absence of the mixture of any *detritus* from the sea, or foreign matter, suggest most forcibly the idea of *perfect repose* at the bottom of the deep sea."‡

Bearing this fact in mind, that there exists a continual pressure of the atmosphere upon the Earth, and associating it with the fact that the Earth is a vast plane "stretched out upon the waters," and it will be seen that it must of necessity slightly fluctuate, or slowly rise and fall in the water. As by the action of the atmosphere the Earth is slowly depressed, the water moves towards the receding shores and produces the flood tide ; and when by the reaction of the resisting oceanic medium the Earth gradually ascends the waters recede, and the ebb tide is produced. This is the *general* cause of tides. Whatever peculiarities are observable they may be traced to the reaction of channels, bays, headlands, and other local causes.

If a raft, or a ship, or any other structure floating upon water be carefully observed, it will be seen to have a gentle fluctuating motion. However calm the water and the atmosphere may be, this gradual rising and falling of the floating mass is always more or less observable. If vessels of different sizes are floating near each other they will be seen to fluctuate with different velocities, the largest and heaviest will move the least rapidly. This motion will be observable whether the vessels be held by their anchors, or moored to buoys, or freely floating in still water. A large and heavily laden vessel will make several fluctuations in a minute of time; the Earth once only in about twelve hours, because it is proportionately larger.

To this simple condition of the Earth, – the action or pressure upon it of the atmosphere, and the reaction or resistance to it of the water, *may he traced* all the leading peculiarities of the tides. The simultaneous ebb and flow upon meridians 180° apart The absence of high and low water in large inland seas and lakes ; which being contained within and fluctuating with the Earth cannot therefore show a relative change in the altitude of the surface. The flux and reflux observed in several inland wells and basins though far from the sea, but being connected with it by subterranean passages, necessarily show a relative difference in the surface levels of the earth and water. And the regular ebb and flood of the water in the great Polar sea recently discovered by Dr. Kane, although it is separated from the great tidal current of the Atlantic Ocean by deep barriers of ice – as will be seen by the following quotation : – "Dr. Kane reported an open sea north of the parallel of 82°. To reach it his party crossed a barrier of ice 80 or 100 miles broad. Before gaining this open water he found the thermometer to show the extreme temperature of – 60°. Passing this icebound region by travelling North, he stood on the shores of an iceless sea extending in an unbroken sheet of water as far as the eye could reach towards the pola Its waves were dashing on the beach with the swell of a boundless ocean. The tides ebbed and flowed in it, and I apprehend that the tidal wave from the Atlantic can no more pass under this icy barrier to be propagated in seas beyond than the vibrations of a musical string can pass with its notes a 'fret' upon which the musician has placed his finger. * * * These tides therefore must have been bom in that cold sea, having their cradle about the North Pole ; and we infer that most, if not all, the unexplored regions about the Pole are covered with deep water ; for, were this unexpected area mostly land, or shallow water, it could not give birth to regular tides."*

That the Earth has a vibratory or tremulous motion, such as must necessarily belong to a floating and fluctuating structure, is abundantly proved by the experience of astronomers and surveyors. If a delicate spirit-level be firmly placed upon a rock or upon the most solid foundation which it is possible to construct, the very curious phenomenon will be observed of constant change in the position of the air-bubble. However carefully the "level" may be adjusted, and the instrument protected from the atmosphere, the "bubble" will not maintain its position many seconds together. A somewhat similar influence has been noticed in astronomical observatories, where instruments of the best construction and placed in the most approved positions cannot always be relied upon without occasional re-adjustment.

SECTION X. Cause of Tides

Notes

* Chambers's Journal, No. 100, p. 379.
* Penny Cyclopædia, Article Sea.
† London Saturday Journal, August 8, 1840, p. 71.
‡ Physical Geography of the Sea, by Lieut. Maury, p. 265.
* *Physical* Geography of the Sea, by Lieut. Maury, p. 176.

SECTION 11

CONSTITUTION, CONDITION, AND ULTIMATE DESTRUCTION OF THE EARTH BY FIRE.

CHEMICAL analysis proves to us the important fact that the great bulk of the Earth – meaning thereby the *land* as distinct from the waters – is composed of metallic oxides or metals in combination with oxygen. When means are adopted to remove the oxygen it is found that most of these metallic bases are highly combustible. The different degrees of affinity existing among the elements of the Earth, give rise to all the rocks, minerals, ores, deposits, and strata which constitute the material habitable world. The different specific gravities or relative densities which these substances are found to possess, and the numerous evidences which exist of their former plastic or semi-fluid condition, afford positive proof that from a once commingled or chaotic state regular but rapid precipitation, stratification, crystillization, and concretion successively occurred ; and that in some way not yet clear to us sufficient chemical action was produced to ignite a great portion of the Earth, and to reduce it to a molten incondescent state, the volatile products of which being forcibly eliminated have broken up the stratified formations, and produced the irregular confused condition which we now observe. That such an incondescent molten state of a great portion of the lower parts of the Earth still exists is a matter of certainty ; and there is evidence that the heat thus internally generated is gradually increasing.

"The uppermost strata of the soil share in all the variations of temperatine which depend upon the seasons ; and this influence is exerted to a depth which, although it varies with the latitude, is never very great Beyond this point the temperature rises in proportion as we descend to greater depths, and it has been shown, by numerous and often-repeated experiments, that the increase of temperature is on average one degree (Fahrenheit) for about every 545 feet Hence it results that at a depth of about twelve miles from the surface, we should be on the verge of an incondescent mass."*

"So great is the heat within the Earth, that in Switzerland, and other countries where the springs of water are very deep, they bring to the surface the warm mineral waters so much used for baths and medicine for the sick ; and it is said, that if you were to dig very deep down into the Earth, the temperature would increase at the rate of one degree of the thermometer for every 100 feet ; so that, at the depth of 7000 feet, or one mile and a half, all the water that you found would be boiling ; and at the depth of about ten miles all the rocks would be melted. * * * A day will yet come when this earth will be burned up by the fire. There is fire, as you have heard, within it, ready to burst forth at any moment."* "This earth, although covered all round with a solid crust, is all on fire within. Its interior is supposed to be a burning mass of melted, glowing

SECTION XI. Constitution, Condition, and ultimate Destruction of the Earth by Fire

metals, fiery gas, and boiling lava. * * * * * The solid crust which covers this inward fire is supposed not to be much more than from 9 to 12 miles in thickness. Whenever this crust breaks open, or is cleft in any place, there rush out lava, fire, melted rocks, fiery gases, and ashes, sometimes in such floods as to bury whole cities. From time to time we read of the earth quaking, trembling, and sometimes opening, and of mountains and small islands (which are mountains in the sea) being thrown up in a day."*

In a periodical called "Recreative Science," at the end of an interesting article on volcanoes, &c., the following sentence occurs : – "The conclusion is therefore inevitable, that the general distribution all over the earth of volcanic vents, their similarity of action and products, their enormous power and seeming inexhaustibility, their extensiveness of action in their respective sites, the continuance of their energies during countless years, and the incessant burning day and night, from year to year, of such craters as Stromboli ; and lastly, the apparent inefficiency of external circumstances in controlling their operations, eruptions happening beneath the sea as beneath the land, in the frigid as in the torrid zone, for these and many less striking phenomena, we must seek for some great and general cause, such only as the central heat of the earth affords us."

Sir Richard Phillips says, "at the depth of 50 feet (from the sea level) the temperature of the earth is the same winter and summer." * * * "The deepest coal mine in England is at Killingworth, near Newcastle-upon-Tyne, and the mean annual temperature at 400 yards below the surface is 77°; and at 300 yards, 70° ; while at the surface it is but 48°, being about one degree of increase for every 15 yards. Hence, at 3,300 yards, the heat would be equal to boiling water, taking 20 yards to a degree. This explains the origin of hot springs. The heat of the Bath waters is 116°, hence they would appear to rise from a depth of 1,320 yards. By experiments made at the Observatory of Paris for ascertaining the increase of temperature from the surface of the earth towards the interior, 51 feet, or 17 yards, corresponds to the increase of one degree Fahrenheit's thermometer. Hence, the temperature of boiling water would be at 8,212 feet, or about 1½ English miles under Paris.'

Professor Silliman, of America, states "that in boring the Artesian wells in Paris, the temperature increased at the rate of 1 degree for every 50 feet downwards ; and, reasoning from causes known to exist, the whole of the interior part of the earth, or, at least, a great part of it, is an ocean of melted rock agitated by violent winds."

Sir Charles Lyell, in his address to the British Association, assembled at Bath, September, 1864, speaking of hot springs generally, said "An increase of heat is always experienced as we descend into the interior of the earth. * * * The estimate deduced by Mr. Hopkins, from an accurate series of observations made in the Monkwearmouth shaft, near Durham, and in the Dukenfield shaft, near Manchester, each of them 2,000 feet in depth. In these shafts the temperature was found to rise at the rate of 1° Fah. for every increase of depth of from 65 to 70 feet."

"The observations made by M. Arago, in 1821, that the deepest Artesian wells are the warmest, threw great light on the origin of thermal springs, and on the establishment of the law, that terrestrial heat increases with increasing depth. It is a remarkable fact, which has but recently been noticed, that at the close of the third century St Patricius, probably Bishop of Partusa, was led to adopt very correct views regarding the phenomenon of the hot springs at Carthage. On being asked what was the cause of boiling water bursting from the earth, he replied, 'Fire is nourished in the clouds, and in the interior of the earth, as Etna and other mountains near Naples may teach you. The subterranean waters rise as if through siphons. The cause of hot springs is this : waters which are more remote from the subterranean fire are colder, whilst those which rise nearer the fire, are heated by it, and bring with them to the surface which we inhabit, an insupportable degree of heat.'"*

The investigations which have been made, and the evidence which has been brought together, render it undeniable that the lower parts of the earth are on fire. Of the intensity of the combustion, no practical idea can be formed. It is fearful beyond comparison. The lava thrown out from a volcano in Mexico, "was so hot that it continued to smoke for twenty years ; and after three years and a half, a piece of wood took fire in it, at a distance of five miles from the crater." In various parts of the world, large islands have been thrown up from the sea, in a red-hot glowing condition, and so intensely heated, that after being forced through many fathoms of salt water, and standing in the midst of it, exposed to wind and rain for several months, they were not sufficiently cooled for persons to approach and stand upon them. "A notable fact is the force exerted in volcanic action, Cotopaxi, in 1738, threw its fiery rockets 3,000 feet above its crater, while in 1744 the blazing mass, struggling for an outlet, roared like a furnace, so that its awful voice was heard at a distance of more than six hundred miles. In 1797, the crater of Tunguragua, one of the great peaks of the Andes, flung out torrents of mud, which dammed up rivers, opened new lakes, and in valleys of a thousand feet wide made deposits six hundred feet deep. The stream from Vesuvius which, in 1737, passed through Torre del Greco, contained thirty-three million cubic feet of solid matter ; and, in 1794, when Torre del Greco was destroyed a second time, the mass of lava amounted to forty-five million cubic feet. In 1669 Etna poured forth a flood which covered 84 square miles of surface, and measured nearly 100,000,000 cubic feet On this occasion the sand and scoriæ formed the Monte Rossi, near Nicolosi, a cone two miles in circumference, and four hundred and fifty feet high. The stream thrown out by Etna, in 1819, was in motion, at the rate of a yard per day, for nine months after the eruption ; and it is on record that the lavas of the same mountain, after a terrible eruption, were not thoroughly cooled and consolidated ten years after the event In the eruption of Vesuvius, A.D. 79, the scoriæ and ashes vomited

SECTION XI. Constitution, Condition, and ultimate Destruction of the Earth by Fire

forth far exceeded the entire bulk of the mountain ; while, in 1660, Etna disgorged more than twenty times its own mass. * * * Vesuvius has thrown its ashes as far as Constantinople, Syria, and Egypt ; it hurled stones eight pounds in weight to Pompeii, a distance of six miles ; while similar masses were tossed up 2,000 feet above its summit Cotopaxi has projected a block one hundred cubic yards in volume a distance of nine miles, while Sum*bawa, in 1815,* during the most terrible eruption on record, sent its ashes as far as Java, a distance of three hundred miles. * * * In viewing these evidences of enormous power, we are forcibly struck with the similarity of action with which they have been associated ; and, carrying our investigation a step further, the same similarity of the producing power is hinted at in the identity of the materials ejected. Thus, if we classify the characteristics of all recorded eruptions, we shall find that the phenomena are all reducible to upheavals of the earth, rumblings and explosions, ejections of carbonic acid, fiery torrents of lava, cinders, and mud, with accompanying thunder and lightning. The last-named phenomena are extrajudicial in character ; they are merely the result of the atmospheric disturbance consequent on the escape of great heat from the earth, just as the burning of an American forest causes thunder and rain. The connection that apparently exists, too, between neighbouring craters is strongly confirmed by the fact that in every distinct volcanic locus but *one* crater is usually active at a time. Since Vesuvius has resumed his activity, the numerous volcanic vents on the other side of the bay have sunk into comparative inactivity ; for ancient writers, who are silent respecting the former, speak of the mephitic vapours of the Lake Avernus as destructive to animal existence, and in earlier days than these Homer pictures the Phlegrean Fields as the entrance to the infernal regions, placed at the limits of the habitable world, unenlightened by rising or setting sun, and enveloped in eternal gloom. * * * * The earth contains within it a mass of heated material ; nay, it is a heated and incandescent body, habitable only because surrounded with a cool crust – the crust being to it a mere shell, within which the vast internal fires are securely inclosed : and yet not securely, perhaps, unless such vents existed as those to which we apply the term volcano. * * * * Every volcano is a safety-valve, ready to relieve the pressure from within when that pressure rises to a certain degree of intensity ; or permanently serving for the escape of conflagrations, which if not so provided with escape, might rend the habitable crust to pieces."*

Thus it is certain, from the phenomena of earthquakes, submarine and inland volcanoes which exist in every part of the earth from the frozen to the tropical regions, hot and boiling springs, fountains of mud and steam, lakes of burning sulphur, jets and blasts of destructive gases, and the choke and fire damps of our coal mines, that at a few miles only below the surface of the earth there exists a vast region of combustion, the intensity and power of which are indescribable, and cannot be compared with anything within the range of human experience.

As the earth is an extended plane resting in and upon the waters of the "great deep" it may fitly be compared to a large vessel or ship floating at anchor, with her "Hold" or lower compartments beneath the water-line filled with burning materials ; and, from our knowledge of the nature and action of fire, it is difficult to understand in what way the combustion can be prevented from extending, when it is known to be surrounded with highly inflammable substances. Wherever a fire is surrounded with heterogeneous materials – some highly combustible and others partially and indirectly combustible – it is not possible for it to remain continually in the same condition nor to diminish in extent and intensity, it must increase and extend itself. That the fire in the earth is so surrounded with inflammable materials is matter of certainty ; the millions of tons of coals, peat, turf, mineral oils, rock tar, pitch, asphalte, bitumen, petroleum, mineral naphtha, and numerous other hydro-carbons which exist in various parts of the earth, and much of these far down below the surface, prove this condition to exist The products of volcanic action being chiefly carbon in combination with hydrogen and oxygen, prove also that these carbon compounds already exist in a state of combustion, and that as such immense quantities of the same fuel still exist, it is quite within the range of possibility that some of the lower strata of combustible matter may take fire and the action rapidly extend itself through the various and innumerable veins which ramify in every direction throughout the whole earth Should such an action commence, knowing, as we do, that the rocks and minerals of the earth are but oxides of inflammable bases, and that the affinities of these bases are greatly weakened and almost suspended in the presence of highly heated carbon, we see clearly that such chemical action or fire would quickly extend and increase in intensity until the whole earth with everything entering into its composition, would rapidly decompose, volatilise, and burst into one vast indescribable, annihilating conflagration !

Notes

* Rambles of a Naturalist, by M. de Quatrefages.
* "The World's Birthday," by Professor Gaussen, Geneva, p. 43.
* "The World's Birthday," by Professor Gaussen, Geneva, *p. 42.*
* "Humboldt's Cosmos," p. 220.
* Recreative Science, p.p. 257 to 260.

SECTION 12.

MISCELLANEA.

MOON'S PHASES. – It has been shown that the Moon is not a reflector of the Sun's light, but is self-luminous. That the luminosity is confined to one-half its surface is sufficiently shown by the fact that at "New Moon" the whole circle or outline of the Moon is often distinctly visible ; but the darker outline is less, or the circle is smaller than the segment which is illuminated From this it is easily seen that "New Moon," "Full Moon," and "Gibbous Moon" are but the different proportions of the illuminated surface which are presented to the observer on earth.

MOON'S APPEARANCE – Astronomers have indulged their imagination to such a degree that the Moon has been considered to be a solid, opaque, spherical world, having mountains, valleys, lakes, volcanic craters, and other conditions analagous to the surface of the earth. So far has this fancy been carried, that the whole visible disc has been mapped out, and special names given to its various peculiarities, as though they had been carefully observed and measured by a party of terrestrial ordnance surveyors. All this has been done in direct opposition to the fect that whoever looks, without previous bias, through a powerful telescope at the Moon's surface, will be puzzled to say what it is really like, or how to compare it with anything known. The comparison which may be made, will depend greatly upon the state of mind of the observer. It is well known that persons looking at the rough bark of a tree, or at the irregular lines or veins in certain kinds of marble and stone, or gazing at the red embers in a dull fire, will, according to the degree of activity of the imagination, be able to see different forms, even the outlines of animals and human feces. It is in this way that persons may fancy that the Moon's surface is broken up into hills and valleys and other arrangements such as are found on earth. But that anything really similar to the surface of our own world is anywhere visible upon the Moon is altogether fallacious. This is admitted by some of those who have written upon the subject "Some persons when they look into a telescope for the first time, having heard that mountains are to be seen, and discovering nothing but these (previously *described)* unmeaning figures, break off in disappointment, and have their faith in these things rather diminished than increased. I would advise, therefore, before the student takes even his *first view* of the Moon through a telescope, to form as clear an idea as he can how mountains, and valleys, and caverns situated at such a distance *ought* to look, and by what marks they may be recognised. Let him seize, if possible, the most favourable periods (about the time of the first quarter), and previously *learn from drawings* and explanations how to *interpret* everything he sees."* "Whenever we exhibit celestial objects to inexperienced observers it is usual to precede the view with good d*rawings* of the objects, accompanied by an explanation of what each appearance exhibited in the telescope *indicates*. The novice is told that mountains and valleys can be seen in the Moon by the aid of the telescope ; but on looking he sees a confused mass of light and shade, and *nothing* which *looks to him like either mountains or valleys !* Had his attention been previously directed to a plain *drawing* of the Moon, and each particular appearance *interpreted* to him, he would then have looked through the telescope with intelligence and satisfaction!"† Thus it is admitted by those who teach that the Moon is a spherical world, having hills and dales like the earth, can only see such things in imagination. "Nothing but unmeaning figures" are really visible, and "the students break off in disappointment, and have their faith in such things rather diminished than increased," "until they previously learn from *drawings* and explanations how to *interpret* everything seen." But who *first made* the drawings ? Who *first interpreted* the "unmeaning figures" and the "confused mass of light and shade ?" Who first declared them to indicate mountains and valleys, and ventured to make drawings and give explanations and interpretations for the purpose of biasing the minds, and fixing or guiding the imaginations of subsequent observers ? Whoever they were, they at least had "given the reins to Fancy," and afterwards took upon themselves to dogmatise and teach their crude and unwarranted imaginings to succeeding investigators. And this is the kind of evidence and "reasoning" which is obtruded in our seats of learning, and spread out in the numerous works which are published for the edification of society !

THE PLANET NEPTUNE – For some years the advocates of the earth's rotundity, and of the Newtonian philosophy generally, were accustomed to refer with an air of pride and triumph to the discovery of a new planet, which was called Neptune, as an undeniable evidence of the truth of their system or theory. The existence of this luminary was said to have been predicated from calculation only, and for a considerable period before it had been seen by the telescope. It was urged that therefore the system which would permit of such a discovery must be true. But the whole matter subsequently proved to be unsatisfactory. That a proper conception may be formed of the actual value of the calculations and their supposed verification, the following account will be useful. "In the year 1781, on March 13, Uranus was discovered by Sir William Herschel, who was examining some small stars near the feet of Gemini; and he observed one of them to have a sensible amount of diameter and less brightness than the others, and it was soon found to be a planet It, however, had been seen before – first, by Flamstead, on December 23rd, 1690 ; and between this time and 1781 it had been observed 16 times by Flamstead, Bradley, Mayer, and Lemonnier ; these astronomers had classed it as a star of the sixth magnitude. Between 1781 and 1820 it was of course very frequently observed ; and it was hoped that at the latter time sufficient data existed to construct accurate tables of its motions. This task was undertaken by M. Bouvard, Member *de L'Academie des Sciences*, but he met with unforeseen difficulties. It was found utterly impossible to construct tables which would represent the 17 ancient observations, and at the same time the more numerous modern ones; and it was finally concluded that the ancient observations were erroneous, or that some strange and unknown action disturbed, or had disturbed, the planet ; consequently M. Bouvard discarded entirely the old observations, and used only those taken between 1781 and 1820, in constructing the tables of Uranus. For some years past it has been found that the tables thus constructed do not agree any better with modern observations, than they do with the ancient observations; *consequently it was evident that the planet was under the influence of some unknown cause.* Several hypotheses have been suggested as to the nature of this cause ; some persons talked of a resisting medium ; others of a great satellite which might accompany Uranus ; some even went so far as to suppose that the vast distance Uranus is from the Sun caused the law of gravitation to lose some of its force ; others thought that the rapid flight of a comet had disturbed its regular movements ; others thought of the existence of a planet beyond Uranus, whose disturbing force caused the anomalous motions of the planet ; but no one did otherwise than follow the bent of his inclination, and did not support his assertion by any positive considerations.

"Thus was the theory of Uranus surrounded with difficulties, when M. Le Verrier, an eminent French mathematician, undertook to investigate the irregularities in its motions. His first paper appeared on the 10th November, 1845, and his second on June 1, 1846 (published in the Comptes Rendûs). In this second paper, after a most elaborate and careful investigation, he proves the utter incompatibility of any of the preceding hypotheses to account for the planet's motions, except only that of the last one, viz., that of a new planet He then successively proves that this planet cannot be situated either between the Sun and Saturn, or between Saturn and Uranus ; but that it must be beyond Uranus. And in this paper he asks the following questions: – 'Is it possible that the irregularities of Uranus can be owing to the action of a planet situated in the ecliptic, at a distance of twice the mean distance of Uranus from the Sun ? If so, where is it actually situated ? What is its mass ? What are the elements of the orbit it describes?"

This was the problem he set himself to work upon, by the means of solving the inverse problem of the perturbations; for instead of having to measure the action of a determined planet, he had to deduce the elements of the orbit of the disturbing planet, and its place in the heavens from the recognised inequalities of Uranus. And this problem M. Le Verrier has successfully solved. In his second paper he deduces the place in the heavens that the body must be as 325° of helio-centric longitude. On the 31st August last he published his third paper. In this he has calculated that the period of the planet is 217 years ; and that it moves in an orbit at the distance of more than 3,000 millions of miles from the Sun ; that its mean longitude on January 1st, 1847, will be 318° 17'; its true longitude 326° 32' ; and that the longitude of its perihelion will be 284° 45' ; that it will appear to have a diameter of 3¼ seconds of arc as seen from the earth ; and that it is now about 5° E. of *Delta Capricorni.*

"These remarkable calculations have pointed out a position which has very nearly proved to be the true one.

"On September 23, Dr. Galle at Berlin discovered a star of the eighth magnitude, which has proved to be the planet. Its place at the time was five degrees from *Delta Capricorni.* It was found to have a disc of 3 seconds as predicted ; and its longitude at the time differs less than a degree from the longitude computed from the above elements. Its daily motion, too, is found to agree very closely with the predicted ; and, judging from this last circumstance, the planet's distance, as stated above, must be nearly the truth.

"Thus the result of these calculations was the discovery of a new planet in the place assigned to it by theory, whose mass, distance, position in the heavens, and orbit it describes round the Sun, were all approximately determined before the planet had ever been seen ; and all agrees with observations, so far as can at present be determined. It is found to have a disc, and its diameter cannot be much less than 40,000 miles, and may be more; its motions are very slow ; it is at present in the constellation of Aquarius as indicated by theory ; and it will be in the constellation of Capricornus all the year 1847. It may be readily seen in a telescope of moderate power.

"Whatever view we take of this noble discovery it is most gratifying, whether at the addition of another planet to our list ; whether at the proving the correctness of the theory of universal gravitation ; or in what view soever, it must be considered as a splendid discovery, and the merit is chiefly due to theoretical astronomy. This discovery is perhaps the greatest triumph of astronomical science that has ever been recorded."*

If such things as criticism, experience, and comparative observation did not exist, the tone of exultation in which the above article indulges might be properly shared in by the astronomical student ; but let the following extracts be carefully read, and it will be seen that such a tone was premature and unwarranted. "Paris, Sept 15, 1848. The only sittings of the Academy of late in which there was anything worth recording, and even this was not of a practical character, were those of the 29th ult. and the 11th inst. On the former day M. Babinet made a communication respecting the planet Neptune, which has been generally called M. Le Verrier's planet, the discovery of it having, as it was said, been made by him from theoretical deductions, which astonished and delighted the scientific public. What M. Le Verrier had inferred from the action on other planets of some body which ought to exist was verified, at least so it was thought at the time, by actual vision. Neptune was actually seen by other astronomers, and the honour of the theorist obtained additional lustra But it appears from a communication of M. Babinet that *this is not the planet* of M. Le Verrier. He had placed his planet at a distance from the Sun equal to thirty-six times the limit of the terrestrial orbit ; Neptune revolves at a distance equal to thirty times of these limits, which makes a difference of nearly *two hundred millions of leagues!* M. Le Verrier had assigned to his planet a body equal to thirty-eight times that of the earth ; Neptune has only *one-third* of this volume M. Le Verrier had stated the revolutions of his planet round the Sun to take place in two hundred and seventeen years; Neptune performs its revolutions in one hundred and sixty-six years! Thus then Neptune is, not M. Le Verrier's planet; and all his theory as regards that planet falls to the ground ! M. Le Verrier may find another planet, but it will not answer the calculations which he had made for Neptune. *In* the sitting of the 14th, M. Le Verrier noticed the communication of M. Babinet, and to a great extent admitted his own error ! He complained indeed that much of what he said was taken in too absolute a sense ; but he evinces much more candour than might have been expected from a disappointed explorer. M. Le Verrier may console himself with the reflection that if he has not been so successful as he thought he had been, others might have been equally unsuccessful, and as he has still before him an immense field for the exercise of observation and calculation, we may hope that he will soon make some discovery which will remove the vexation of his present disappointment."*

"As the data of Le Verrier and Adams stand at present there is a discrepancy between the predicted and the true distance ; and in some other elements of the planet It remains, therefore, for these or future astronomers to reconcile theory with fact ; or, perhaps, as in the case of Uranus, to make the new planet the means of leading to yet greater discoveries. It would appear, from the most recent observations, that the mass of Neptune, instead of being as at first stated one nine thousand three hundredth is only one twenty three thousandth that of the Sun ; whilst its periodic time is now given with a greater probability at 166 years ; and its mean distance from the Sun nearly thirty. Le Verrier gave the mean distance from the Sun thirty-six times that of the Earth; and the period of revolution 217 years.*

"May 14, 1847. A Paper was read before the Royal Astronomical Society, by Professer Schumacher, 'on the identity of the planet Neptune (M. le Verrier's) with a star observed by M. Lalande in May, 1795.'"†

Such mistakes as the above ought at least to make the advocates of the Newtonian theory less positive, and more ready to acknowledge that at best their system is but hypothetical and must sooner or later give place to a philosophy the premises of which are demonstrable, and which is in all its details sequent and consistent

ZETETIC ASTRONOMY. EARTH NOT A GLOBE!

PENDULUM EXPERIMENTS AS PROOFS OF EARTH'S MOTION.

IN the early part of the year 1851, the scientific journals and nearly all the newspapers published in Great Britain and on the Continents of Europe and America were occupied in recording and discussing certain experiments with the pendulum, first made by M. Foucault, of Paris ; and the public were startled by the announcement that the results furnished a practical proof of the Earth's rotation.

The subject was referred to in the *Literary Gazette*, in the following words : – "Everybody knows what is meant by a pendulum in its simplest form, a weight hanging by a thread to a fixed point. Such was the pendulum experimented upon long ago by Galileo, who discovered the well-known law of isochronous vibrations, applicable to the same. The subject has since received a thorough examination, as well theoretical as practical, from mathematicians and mechanicians ; and yet, strange to say, the most remarkable feature of the phenomenon has remained unobserved and wholly unsuspected until within the last few weeks, when a young and promising French physicist, M. Foucault, who was induced by certain reflections to repeat Galileo's experiments in the cellar of his mother's house at Paris, succeeded in establishing the existence of a fact connected with it which gives an immediate and visible demonstration of the Earth's rotation. Suppose the pendulum already described to be set moving in a vertical plane from north to south, the plane in which it vibrates, to ordinary observation, would appear to be stationary. M. Foucault, however, has succeeded in showing that this is not the case, but that the plane is itself slowly moving round the fixed point as a centre in a direction contrary to the Earth's rotation, *i.e.*, with the apparent heavens, from east to west. His experiments have since been repeated in the hall of the observatory, under the superintendence of M. Arago, and fully confirmed. If a pointer be attached to the weight of a pendulum suspended by a long and fine wire, capable of turning round in all directions, and nearly in contact with the floor of a room, the line which this pointer appears to trace on the ground, and which may easily be followed by a chalk mark, will be found to be slowly, but visibly, and constantly moving round, like the hand of a watch dial ; and the least consideration will show that this ought to be the case, and will excite astonishment that so simple a consequence as this is, of the most elementary laws of Geometry and Mechanics, should so long have remained unobserved. * * * The subject has created a great sensation in the mathematical and physical circles of Paris. It is proposed to obtain permission from the Government to carry on further observations by means of a pendulum suspended from the dome of the Pantheon, length of suspension being a desideratum in order to make the result visible on a larger scale, and secure greater constancy and duration in the experiment The time required for the performance of a complete revolution of the plane of vibration would be about 32 hours 8 minutes for the parallel of Paris

SECTION XII. Miscellanea

; 30 hours 40 minutes for that of London ; and at 30 degrees from the equator exactly 48 hours. Certainly any one who should have proposed not many weeks back to prove the rotation of the Earth upon which we stand by means of direct experiment made upon its surface would have run the risk, with the mob of gentlemen who write upon mechanics, of being thought as mad as if he were to have proposed reviving Bishop Wilkins's notable plan for going to the North American colonies in a few hours, by rising in a balloon from the Earth and gently floating in the air until the Earth, in its diurnal rotation, have turned the desired quarter towards the suspended æronaut, whereupon as gently to descend ; so necessary and wholesome is it occasionally to reconsider the apparently simplest and best established conclusions of science."

The following is from the *Scotsman,* which has always been distinguished for the accuracy of its scientific papers. The article bears the initials "C. M.," which will at once be recognised as those of Mr. Charles Maclaren, for many years the accomplished editor of that journal : – "The beautiful experiment contrived by M. Foucault to demonstrate the rotation of the globe, has deservedly excited univeral interest. * * * A desire has always been felt that some method could be devised of rendering this rotation palpable to the senses. Even the illustrious Laplace participated in this feeling and has left it on record. 'Although,' he says, ' the rotation of the Earth is now established with all the certainty which the physical sciences require, still a direct proof of that phenomenon ought to interest both geometricians and astronomers.' *No* man ever knew the laws of the planetary motions better than Laplace, and before penning such a sentence, it is probable that he had turned the subject in his mind, and without discovering any process by which the object could be attained ; but it does not follow that if he had applied the whole force of his genius to the task, he would not have succeeded. Be this as it may, here we have the problem solved by a man not probably possessing a tithe of his science or talent ; and, what is very remarkable, after the discovery was made, it was found to be legitimately deducible from mathematical principles. * * * In this, as in many other cases, the *fact* comes first, and takes us by surprise ; after which we find that we had long been in possession of the principles from which it flowed, and that, with the clue we had in our hands, theory should have revealed the fact to us long before. M. Foucalt's communication describing his experiments is in the *Comptes Rendus* of the Academy of Sciences, for 3rd February, 1851. His first experiments were made with a pendulum only two metres (6ft. 6¼in.) in length, consisting of a steel wire from 6-10ths to 11-10ths of a millimetre in diameter (the millimetre is the 25th part of an inch) ; to the lower end of which was attached a polished brass ball, weighing 5 kilogrammes, or 11 English pounds. * * * A metallic point projecting below the ball, and so directed as if it formed a continuation of the suspension wire, served as an index to mark the change of position more precisely. The pendulum hung from a steel plate in such a manner as to move freely in any vertical plane. To start the oscillatory movement without giving the ball any bias, it was drawn to one side with a cord, which held the ball by a loop ; the cord was then burned, after which the loop fell off, and the vibrations (generally limited to an arc of 15 or 20 degrees) commenced. In one minute the ball had sensibly deviated from the original plane of vibration towards the observer's left. Afterwards he experimented at the Observatory with a pendulum 11 metres (30 feet) long, and latterly at the Pantheon with one still longer. The advantage of a large pendulum, as compared with a small one, is, that a longer time elapses before it comes to a state of rest ; for machinery cannot be employed here, as in a clock, to continue the motion. The pendulum is suspended over the centre of a circular table, whose circumference is divided into degrees and minutes. The vibrations are begun in the manner above described, and in a short time it is observed that the pendulum, instead of returning to the same point of the circle from *which* it started, has shifted to the left. If narrowly observed, the change in the plane of vibration (says M. Foucault) is perceptible in one minute, and in half an hour, "Ille sante aux yeux," it is quite palpable. At Paris the change exceeds 11 degrees in an hour. Thus, supposing the oscillations to commence in a plane directed south and north, in two hours the oscillations will point SSW. and NNE.; in four hours they will point SW. and NE.; and in eight hours the oscillations will point due east and west, or at right angles to their original direction. To a spectator the change seems to be in the pendulum, which, without any visible cause, has shifted round a quarter of a circle ; but the real change is in the table, which, resting on the Earth, and accompanying it in its rotation, has performed a fourth (and something more) of its diurnal revolution.

    No one anticipated such a result; and the experiment has been received by some with incredulity, by all with wonderment ; and one source of the incredulity arises from the difficulty of conceiving how, amidst the ten thousand experiments of which the pendulum has been the subject, so remarkable a fact could have escaped notice so long. Fully admitting that these experiments have generally been conducted with pendulums which had little freedom of motion horizontally, we still think it odd that somebody did not stumble upon the curious fect. Though all the parts of the Earth complete their revolution in the same space of time, it is found that the rate of horizontal motion in Foucault's pendulum varies with the latitude of the place where the experiment is made. At the pole, the pendulum would pass over 15 degrees in an hour, like the Earth itself, and complete its circuit in 24 hours. At Edinburgh, the pendulum would pass over 12½ degrees in an hour, and would complete its revolution in 29 hours 7 minutes. At Paris, the rate of motion is 11 degrees and 20 minutes per hour, and the revolution should be completed in 32 hours.

SECTION XII. Miscellanea

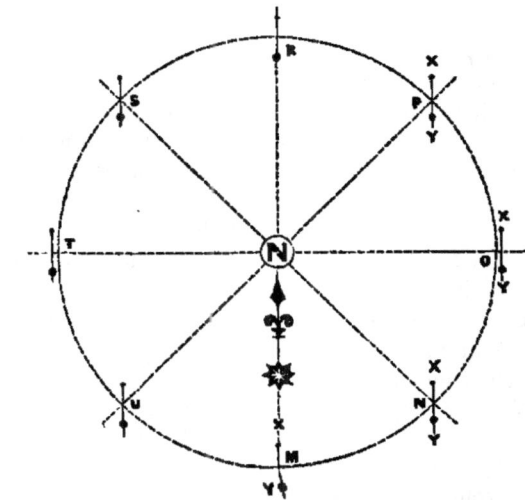

Let the above figure represent a portion of the Earth's surface near the north pole N. Suppose the pendulum to be set in motion at m, so as to vibrate in the direction $x\,y$, which coincides with that of the meridian m N or m r. The Earth in the meantime is pursuing its easterly course, and the meridian line m N has come in six hours into the position n N. It has been hitherto supposed that the pendulum would now vibrate in the new direction n N, assumed by the meridian, but thanks to M. Foucault, we now know that this is a mistake. The pendulum will vibrate in a plane $x\,n\,y$, parallel to its original plane at m, as will be manifest if the plane of vibration points to some object in absolute space, such as a star. While the meridian line m N will in the course of 24 hours range round the whole circle of the heavens, and point successively in the direction n N, o N, p N, r N, 8 N, t N, and u N, the pendulum's plane of vibration $x\,y$, whether at m, at n, at o, at p, at r, at 8, at t, or at u, will always be parallel to itself, pointing invariably to the same star, and were a circular table placed under the pendulum, its plane of vibration, while really stationary, would appear to perform a complete revolution.

This stationary position of the plane of vibration at the pole seems to present little difficulty. We impress a peculiar motion on the pendulum in setting it a going The Earth is at the same time carrying the pendulum eastward, but *at the pole* the one motion will not interfere with the other. The only action of the Earth on the pendulum there is that of attracting it towards its own (the Earth's) centre. But this attraction is exactly in the plane of vibration and merely tends to continue the oscillatory motion without disturbing it It is otherwise if the experiment is made at some other point, say 20 degrees distant from the pole. Supposing the vibrations to commence in the plane of the meridian, then as the tendency of the pendulum is to continue its vibrations in planes absolutely parallel to the original plane, it will be seen, if we trace both motions, that, while it is carried eastward with the Earth along a parallel of latitude, this tendency will operate to draw the plane of vibration away from a 'great circle' into a 'small circle' (that is, from a circle dividing the globe into two *equal* parts, into one dividing it into two *unequal* parts). But the pendulum *must* necessarily move in a 'great circle,' and hence to counteract its tendency to deviate into a ' small circle,' a correctory movement is constantly going on, to which the lengthening of the period necessary to complete a revolution must be ascribed. At Edinburgh the period is about 29 hours, at Paris 32, at Cairo 48, at Calcutta 63. At the Equator, the period stretches out to infinity. M. Foucault's rule is, that the angular space passed over by the pendulum at any latitude in a given time, is equal to the angular motion of the Earth in the period, multiplied by the sine of the latitude. The angular motion of the Earth is 15 degrees per hour ; and at the latitude of 30, for example, the sine being to radius as 500 to 1000, the angular motion of the pendulum will consequently be 7½ degrees per hour. It is, therefore, easily found. It follows that the motions of the pendulum may be employed in a rough way to indicate the latitude of a place."*

Notwithstanding the apparent certainty of these pendulum experiments, and the supposed exactitude of the conclusions deducible there-from, many of the same school of philosophy differed with each other, remained dissatisfied, and raised very serious objections both to the value of the experiments themselves, and to the supposed proof which they furnished of the Earth's rotation. One writer in the *Times* newspaper of the period, who signs himself "B. A. C.," says, "I have read the accounts of the Parisian experiment as they have appeared in many of our papers, and must confess that I still remain unconvinced of the reality of the phenomenon. It appears to me that, except at the pole where the point of suspension is immovable, no result can be obtained. In other cases the shifting of the direction of passage through the lowest point that takes place during an excursion of the pendulum, from that point in one direction and its return to it again, will be exactly compensated by the corresponding shifting in the contrary direction during the pendulum's excursion on the opposite side. Take a particular case. Suppose the pendulum in any latitude to be set oscillating in the meridian plane, and to be started from the vertical towards the south. It is obvious that the wire by which it is suspended *does not continue to describe a plane,* but a species of conoidal surface ; that when the pendulum has reached its extreme point its direction is to the south-west, and that as the tangent plane to the described surface through the point of suspension necessarily contains the normal to the Earth at the same point, the pendulum on its return passes through the same point in the direction north-east. Now, starting again from this point, we have exactly the circumstances of the last case, the primary plane being shifted slightly out of the meridian ; when, therefore, the pendulum has reached its extreme point of excursion the direction of the wire is to the west of this plane, and when it returns to the vertical the direction of passage through the lowest point is as much to the west of this plane as it was in the former case to the west of the meridian plane ; but since it is now moving from north to south instead of from south to north, as in the former case, its former deviation receives complete compensation, and the primary plane returns again to the meridian, when the whole process recurs."

In the *Liverpool Mercury* of May 23, 1851, the following letter appeared : – "The supposed manifestation of the Rotation of the Earth. – The French, English, and European continental journals have given publicity to an experiment made in Paris with a pendulum ; which experiment is said to have had the same results when made elsewhere. To the facts set forth no contradiction has been given, and it is therefore to be hoped that they are true. The correctness of the inferences drawn from the facts is another matter. The first position of these theorists is, that in a complete vacuum beyond the sphere of the Earth's atmosphere, a pendulum will continue to oscillate in one and the same original plane. On that supposition their whole theory is founded. In making this supposition the fact is overlooked that there is *no vibratory motion* unless through atmospheric resistance, or by force opposing impulse. Perpetual progress in rectilinear motion may be imagined, as in the corpuscular theory of light ; circular motion may also be found in the planetary systems ; and parabolic and hyperbolic motions in those of comets ; but vibration is artificial and of limited duration. No body in nature returns the same road it went, unless artificially constrained to do so. The supposition of a permanent vibratory motion such as is presumed in the theory advanced, is *unfounded in fact,* and absurd in idea ; and the whole affair of this proclaimed discovery falls to the ground. It is what the French call a 'mystification' – anglice a 'humbug.' Liverpool, 22nd May, 1851." "T."

Another writer declared that he and others had made many experiments and had discovered that the plane of vibration had nothing whatever to do with the meridian longitude nor with the Earth's motion, but followed the plane of the magnetic meridian.

"A scientific gentleman in Dundee recently tried the pendulum experiment, and he says – 'that the pendulum is capable of showing the Earth's motion I regard as a *gross delusion;* but that it tends to the *magnetic meridian* I have found to be a fact.'"*

In many cases the experiments have not shown a change at all in the plane of oscillation of the pendulum ; in others the alteration in the plane of vibration has been in the *wrong direction ;* and very often the *rate of variation* has been altogether different to that which theory indicated. The following is a case in illustration : – "On Wednesday evening the Rev. H. H. Jones, F.R.A.S , exhibited the apparatus of Foucault to illustrate the diurnal rotation of the Earth, in the Library Hall of the Manchester Athenaeum. The preparations were simple. A circle of chalk was drawn in the centre of the floor, immediately under the arched skylight The circle was exactly 360 inches in its circumference, every inch being intended to represent one degree According to a calculation Mr. Jones had made, and which he produced at the Philosophical Society six weeks ago, the plane of oscillation of the pendulum would, at Manchester, diverge about one degree in five minutes, or perhaps a very little less. He therefore drew this circle exactly 360 inches round, and marked the inches on its circumference. The pendulum was hung from the skylight immediately over the centre of the circle, the point of suspension being 25 feet high. At that length of wire, it should require 2½ seconds to make each oscillation across the circle. The brazen ball, which at the end of a fine wire constituted the pendulum, was furnished with a point, to enable the spectator to observe the more easily its course. A long line was drawn through the diameter of the circle, due north and south, and the pendulum started so as to swing exactly along this line ; to the westward of which, at intervals of three inches at the circumference, two other lines were drawn, passing through the centre. According to the theory, the pendulum should diverge from its original line towards the west, at the rate of one inch or degree in five minutes. This, however, Mr. Jones explained, was a perfection of accuracy only attainable in a vacuum, and rarely could be approached where the pendulum had to pass through an atmosphere subject to disturbances; besides, it was difficult to avoid giving it some slight lateral bias at starting. In order to obviate this as much as possible, the steel wire was as fine as would bear the weight, 1-30th of an inch thick ; and the point of suspension was adjusted with delicate nicety. An iron bolt was screwed into the frame-work of the skylight ; into it a brass nut was inserted – the wire passed through the nut (the hollow sides of which were bell-shaped, in order to give it fair play), and at the top the wire ended in a globular piece, there being also a fine screw to keep it from slipping. * * * The pendulum was gently drawn up to one side, at the southern end of the diametrical line, and attached by a thread to something near. When it hung quite still the thread was burnt asunder, and the pendulum began to oscillate to and fro across the circle. * * * Before it had been going on quite seven minutes, it had reached nearly the third degree towards the west, whereas it *ought* to have occupied a quarter of an hour in getting thus far from its starting line, even making no allowance for the resistance of the atmosphere."*

Besides the irregularities so often observed in the time and direction of the pendulum vibrations, and which are quite sufficient to render them worthless as evidence of the Earth s motion, the use which the Newtonian astronomers made of the general fact that the plane of oscillation is variable, was most unfair and illogical. It was proclaimed to the world as a visible proof of the Earth s diurnal motion ; but the motion was *assumed to exist*, and then employed to explain the cause of the fact which was first called a proof of the thing assumed! A greater violation of the laws of investigation was never perpetrar ted ! The whole subject as developed and applied by the theoretical philosophers is to the fullest degree unreasonable and absurd – not a "jot or tittle" better than the reasoning contained in the following letter : – "Sir, – Allow me to call your serious and polite attention to the extraordinary phenomenon, demonstrating the rotation of the Earth, which I at this present moment experience, and you yourself or anybody else, I have not the slightest doubt, would be satisfied of, under similar circumstances. Some sceptical and obstinate individuals may doubt that the Earth's motion is visible, but I say from personal observation its a positive fact I don't care about latitude or longitude, or a vibratory pendulum revolving round the sine of a tangent on a spherical surface, nor axes, nor apsides, nor anything of the sort. That is all rubbish. AU I know is, I see the ceiling of this coffee-room going round. I perceive this distinctly with the naked eye – only my sight has been sharpened by a slight stimulant I write alter my sixth go of brandy-and water, whereof witness my hand," – "Swiggins" – *Goose and Gridiron, May 5, 1851.* – "P.S. Why do two waiters come when I only call one?" *

The whole matter as handled by the astronomical theorists is fully deserving of the ridicule implied in the above quotation from *Punch* ; but because great ingenuity has been shewn, and much thought and devotion manifested in connection with it, and the general public thereby greatly deceived, it is necessary that the subject should be fairly and seriously examined. What are the facts ?

First – When a pendulum, constructed according to the plan of M. Foucault, is allowed to vibrate, its plane of vibration is often variable – *not always.* The variation when it *does* occur, is *not uniform* – is not always the same in the same place ; nor always the same either in its rate or velocity, or in its direction. It cannot therefore be taken as evidence ; for that which is inconstant cannot be used in favour of or against any given proposition. It therefore *is not evidence and proves nothing !*

Secondly. – If the plane of vibration *is* observed to change, where is the connection between such change and the supposed motion of the Earth ? What principle of reasoning guides the experimenter to the conclusion that it is the Earth which moves underneath the pendulum, and not the pendulum which moves over the Earth ? What logical right or necessity forces one conclusion in preference to the other ?

Thirdly. – Why was not the peculiar arrangement of the point of suspension of the pendulum specially considered, in regard to its possible influence upon the plane of oscillation ? Was it not known, or was it overlooked, or was it, in the climax of theoretical revelry, ignored that a "ball-and-socket" joint is one which facilitates *circular* motion more readily than any other ? and that a pendulum so suspended (as was M. Foucault's), could not, after passing over one arc of vibration, return through the same arc without there being many chances to one that its globular point of suspension would slightly turn or twist in its bed, and therefore give to the return or backward oscillation a slight change of direction ? Let the *immediate cause* of the pendulum's liability to change its plane of vibration be traced ; and it will be found not to have the slightest connection with the motion or non-motion of the surface over which it vibrates.

At a recent meeting of the French Academy of sciences, "M. Dehaut sent in a note, stating that M. Foucault (whose experiments on the pendulum effected a few years ago at the Pantheon, are of European notoriety) is not the first discoverer of the fact that the plane of oscillation of the free pendulum is invariable; but that the honour of the discovery is due to Poinsinet de Sivry, who, in 1782, stated, in a note to his translation of 'Pliny,' that a mariner's compass might be constructed without a magnet, by making a pendulum and setting it in motion in a given direction ; because, provided the motion were continually kept up, the pendulum would continue to oscillate in the same direction, no matter by how many points, or how often the ship might happen to change her coursa."

Notes

* "Mechanism of the Heavens," by Denison Olmsted, LL.D., Professor of Natural Philosophy and Astronomy in Gale College, U.S.
† *Mitchell's* "Orbs of Heaven," p. 232.
* "Illustrated London Almanack for 1847."
* "Times" Newspaper, Monday, Sept. 18, 1848.
* "Cosmos," by Humboldt, p. 75.
† "Report of Royal Astronomical Society," for Feb. 11, 1848, No. 4, vol. 8.
* Supplement of the *Manchester Examiner,* of May 24, 1851.
* *Liverpool Journal*, May 17, 1851.
* "Manchester Examiner" (Supplement), May 24, 1851.
* "Punch," May 10, 1851.

SECTION 13.

PERSPECTIVE ON THE SEA.

It has been shown (at pages 25 to 34) that the law of perspective, as commonly taught in our Schools of Art, is fallacious and contrary to everything seen in nature. If an object be held up in the air, and gradually carried away from an observer who maintains his position, it is true that all its parts will converge to one and the same point ; but if the same object be placed upon the ground and similarly moved away from a fixed observer, the same predicate is false. In the first case the *centre* of the object is the *datum* to which every point of the exterior converges ; but in the second case the *ground* becomes the *datum*, in and towards which every part of the object converges in succession, beginning with the lowest, or that nearest to it.

Instances: – A man with light trousers and black boots walking along a level path, will appear at a certain distance as though the boots had been removed, and the trousers brought in contact with the ground.

À young girl, with short garments terminating ten or twelve inches above the feet, will, in walking forward, appear to sink towards the Earth, the space between which and the bottom of the clothes will appear to gradually diminish, and in the distance of half-a-mile the limbs, which were first seen for ten or twelve inches, will be invisible – the bottom of the garment will seem to touch the ground

A small dog running along will appear to gradually shorten by the legs, which, in less than half a mile, will be invisible, and the body appear to glide upon the earth.

Horses and cattle moving away from a given point will seem to have lost their hoofs, and to be walking upon the outer bones of the limbs.

Carriages similarly receding will seem to lose that portion of the rim of the wheels which touches the Earth ; the axles will seem to get lower ; and at the distance of a few miles, the body will appear to drag along in contact with the ground. This is very remarkable in the case of a railway carriage when moving away upon a straight and level portion of line several miles in length. These instances, which are but a few of what might be quoted, will be sufficient to prove, beyond the power of doubt or the necessity for controversy, that upon a plane or horizontal surface, the *lowest part* of bodies receding from a given point of observation will disappear *before ike higher*. This is precisely what is observed in the case of a ship at sea, when outward bound – the *lowest* part – the hull, disappearing before the higher parts – the sails and mast head. Abstractedly, when the lowest part of a receding object thus disappears by entering the "vanishing point," it could be seen again to any and every extent by a telescope, if the power were sufficient to magnify at the distance observed. This is to a great extent practicable upon smooth horizontal surfaces, as upon frozen lakes or canals ; and upon long straight lines of railway. But the power of restoring such objects is greatly modified and diminished where the surface is undulating or otherwise moveable, as in large and level meadows, and pasture lands generally ; in the vast prairies and grassy plains of America ; and especially so upon the ocean, where the surface is always more or less in an undulating condition. In Holland and other level countries, persons have been seen in winter, skating upon the ice, at distances varying from ten to twenty miles. On some of the straight and "level" lines of railway which cross the prairies of America, the trains have been observed for more than twenty miles ; but upon the sea the conditions are altered, and the hull of a receding vessel can only be seen for a few miles, and this will depend very greatly – the altitude of the observer being the same, upon the state of the water. When the surface is calm, the hull may be seen much farther than when it is rough and stormy ; but under ordinary circumstances, when to the naked eye the hull has just become invisible, or is doubtfully visible, it may be seen again distinctly by the aid of a powerful telescope. Although abstractedly or mathematically there should be no limit to this power of restoring by a telescope a lost object upon a smooth horizontal surface, upon the sea this limit is soon observed ; the water being variable in its degree of agitation, the limit of sight over its surface is equally variable, as shown by the following experiments: – In May, 1864, on several occasions when the water was unusually calm, from the landing stairs of the Victoria pier at Portsmouth, and from an elevation of 2ft. 8in. above the water, the greater part of the hull of the Nab Light-ship was, through a good telescope, distinctly visible ; but on other experiments being made, when the water was less calm, no portion of it could be seen from the same elevation, notwithstanding that the most powerful telescopes were employed. At other times half the hull, and sometimes only the upper part of the bulwarks, were visible. If the hull had been invisible from the rotundity of the Earth, the following calculation will show that it should at all times have been 24 feet below the horizon : – The distance of the light-ship from the pier is 8 statute miles. The elevation of the observer being 32 inches above the water, would require 2 miles to be deducted as the distance of the supposed convex horizon ; for the square of 2 multiplied by 8 inches (the fall in the first mile of the Earth s curvation) equals 32 inches. This deducted from the 8 miles, will leave 6 miles as the distance from the horizon to the light ship. Hence $6^2 \times 8$ in. = 288 inches, or 24 feet The top of the bulwarks, it was said, rose about 10 ft. above the water line ; hence, deducting 10 from 24 feet, under all circumstances, even had the water been perfectly smooth and stationary, the top of the hull should have been 14 feet below the summit of the arc of water, or beneath the line of sight ! This one fact is entirely fatal to the doctrine of the Earth's rotundity. But such facts have been observed in various other places – the north-west light-ship in Liverpool Bay, and the light vessels of many other channels near the southern, eastern, and western shores of Great Britain. From the beach of Southsea

SECTION XIII. Perspective on the Sea

Common, near Portsmouth, the observer lying down near the water, above the surface of which the eye was 2½ feet, and with a telescope looking across Spithead to the quarantine ship lying in the "Roads," between Ryde and Cowes, in the Isle of Wight, a distance of 7 miles, the copper sheathing of that vessel was distinctly seen, the depth of which was about 2 feet Making the usual calculation in accordance with the doctrine of the Earth's convexity, it will be seen that an arc of water ought to have existed between the two points, the summit of which arc should have been 16 feet above the copper sheathing of the vessel !

From an elevation of 2½ feet above the water opposite the Royal Yacht Club House, in West Cowes, Isle of Wight, the pile work and promenade of the pier at Stoke's Bay, near Gosport, and nearly opposite Osborne House, were easily distinguished through various telescopes : the distance is 7 miles, the altitude of the promenade 10 feet, and the usual calculation will show that this pier ought to have been many feet below the horizon !

It is a well-known fact that the light of the Eddystone lighthouse is often plainly visible from the beach in Plymouth Sound ; and sometimes, when the sea is very calm, persons can see it distinctly when sitting in ordinary rowing boats in that part of the Sound which will allow the line of sight to pass between Drake's Island and the western end of the Breakwater. The distance is 14 statute miles. In a list of lighthouses in a work called "The Lighthouses of the World,' by A. G. Findlay, F.R.G.S., published in 1862, by Richard H. Lawrie, 53, Fleet Street, London, it is said, at page 28 : – "In the Tables the height of the flame above the highest tide high water level is given, so that it is the *minimum* range of the light ; to this elevation 10 feet is added for the height of the deck of the ship above the sea. Besides the increased distance to which low water will cause the light to be seen, the effect of refraction will also sometimes increase their range." In the "Tables" above referred to, at page 36 the Eddystone light is said to be visible 13 miles. But these 13 miles are nautical measure ; and as 3 nautical miles equal 3½ statute miles, the distance at which the Eddystone light is visible is over 15 statute miles. Notwithstanding that the Eddystone light is actually visible at a distance of 15 statute miles, and admitted to be so both by the Admiralty authorities and by calculation according to the doctrine of rotundity, very often at the same distance, the lantern is not visible at an elevation of 4 feet from the water; showing that the law of perspective, previously referred to, is greatly influenced by the state of the surface of the water over which the line of sight is directed. A remarkable illustration of this influence is given in the *Western* Daily Mercury, published in Plymouth, of October 25, 1864. Several discussions had previously taken place at the Plymouth Athenæum and the Devonport Mechanics' Institute, on the true figure of the Earth ; subsequent to which a committee was formed for the purpose of making experiments bearing on the question at issue. The names of the gentlemen as given in the above-named journal were "Parallax" (the author of this work), "Theta" (Mr. Henry, a teacher in Her Majesty's Dock-yard, Devonport), and Messrs. Osborne, Richards, Rickard, Mogg, Evers, and Pearce, all of Plymouth From the report published as above stated, the following quotation is made : – Observation 6th: "*On the beach, at 5 feet from the water level, the Eddystone was entirely out of sight.*"

The matter may be summarized as follows : – At any time when the sea is calm and the weather clear, the Light of the Eddystone, which is 89 feet above the foundation on the rock, may be distinctly seen from an elevation of 5 feet above the water level ; according to the Admiralty directions, it "may be seen 13 nautical (or 15 statute) miles,"* or one mile still farther away than the position of the observers on the above-named occasion ; and yet *on that occasion,* and at a distance of only 14 statute miles, notwithstanding that it was a very fine autumn day, and a clear back ground existed, not only was the lantern, which is 89 feet high, not visible, but the *top of the vane,* which is 100 feet above the foundation was, as stated in the report, "*entirely out of sight.*"

That vessels and lighthouses are sometimes more distinctly seen than at others; and that the lower parts of such objects are sooner lost sight of when the sea is rough than when it is calm, are items in the experience of seafaring people as common as their knowledge of the changes in the weather ; and prominence is only given here to the above case because it was verified by persons of different opinions upon the subject of the Earth's form, and in the presence of several hundreds of the most learned and respectable inhabitants of Plymouth and the neighbourhood. The conclusion which such observations necessitate and force upon us is, that the law of perspective which is everywhere visible on land, is *modified* when observed in connection with objects upon or near the sea. But *how* modified ? If the water of the ocean were frozen and at perfect rest, any object upon its surface would be seen as far as telescopic or magnifying power could be brought to bear upon it But because this is not the case – because the water is always more or less in motion, not only of progression but of fluctuation, the swells and waves, into which the surface is broken operate to prevent the line of sight from passing parallel to the horizontal surface of the water. It has been shown at pages 16 to 20, and also at 25 to 33, that the surface of the Earth and Sea appears to rise up to the level, or altitude of the eye ; and that at a certain distance the line of sight and the surface which is parallel to it appear to converge to a "vanishing point;" which point is "the horizon." If this horizon, or vanishing point, were formed by the apparent junction of two *perfectly stationary* parallel lines, it could be penetrated by a telescope of sufficient power to magnify at the distance ; but because upon the sea the surface of the water is *not stationary,* the line of sight at the vanishing point becomes angular instead of parallel, and telescopic power is of little avail in restoring objects beyond this point The following diagram will render this clear : – The hori

SECTION XIII. Perspective on the Sea

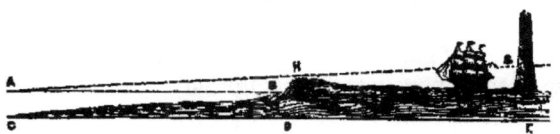

zontal line C D E and the line of sight A B are parallel to each other, and appear to meet at the vanishing point B. But at and about this point the line A B is intercepted by the undulating, or fluctuating surface of the water ; the degree of which is variable, being sometimes very great and at others inconsiderable, and having to pass over the crest of the waves, as at H, is obliged to become A H, instead of A B, and will therefore fall upon a ship, lighthouse, or other object at the point S, or higher or lower as such objects are more or less beyond the point H.

It is worthy of note that the waves at the point H, whatever their real magnitude may be, are *magnified* and rendered more obstructive by the very instrument – the telescope – which is employed to make the objects beyond more plainly visible: and thus the phenomenon is often very strikingly observed – that while a powerful telescope will render the sails and rigging of a ship when beyond the point H, or the optical horizon, so distinct that the very ropes are easily distinguished, not the slightest portion of the hull can be seen. The "crested waters" form a barrier to the horizontal line-of-sight, as substantial as would the summit of an intervening rock or island.

In the report which appeared in the *Western Daily Mercury*, of Oct. 25, 1864, the following observations were also recorded : – "On the seafront of the Camera house, and at an elevation of 110 feet from the mean level of the sea, a plane mirror was fixed, by the aid of a plumb-line, in a *true vertical position*. In this mirror the distant horizon was distinctly visible on a level with the eye of the observer. This was the simple fact, as observed by the several members of the committee which had been appointed. But some of the observers remarked that the line of the horizon in the mirror rose and fell with the eye, as also did every thing else which was reflected, and that this ought to be recorded as an *addendum* – granted. The surface of the sea appeared to regularly ascend from the base of the Hoe to the distant horizon. The horizon from the extreme east to the west, as far as the eye could see, was parallel to a horizontal line."

The following version was recorded in the same journal, of the same date, and was furnished by one of the committee who had manifested a very marked aversion to the doctrine that the surface of all water is horizontal : – "A vertical looking-glass was suspended from the Camera and the horizon seen in it, as well as various other objects reflected, rising and falling with the eye. The water was seen in the glass to ascend from the base of the Hoe to the horizon. The horizon appeared parallel to a horizontal line."

It will be observed that the two reports are substantially the same, and very strongly corroborate the remarks made at pages 15, 16, and 17 of this work. Indeed no other report could have been given without the author's becoming subject to the charge of glaring, obstinate, and wilful misrepresentation. What then has again been demonstrated? That the surface of all water *is horizontal,* and that, therefore, the Earth cannot possibly be anything other than a Plane. All appearances to the contrary have been shown to be purely optical and adventitious.

Another proof that the surface of all water is horizontal and that therefore the Earth cannot be a globe is furnished by the following experiment, which was made in May, 1864, on the new pier at Southsea, near Portsmouth : – A telescope was fixed upon a stand and directed across the water at Spithead to the pier head at Ryde, in the Isle of Wight, as shown in the subjoined diagram. The line of sight crossed a certain

part of the funnel of one of the regular steamers trading between Portsmouth and the Isle of Wight ; and it was observed to cut or fall upon the same part during the whole of the passage to Ryde Pier, thus proving that the water between the two piers is horizontal, because it was parallel to the line of sight from the telescope fixed at Southsea. If the Earth were a globe the channel between Ryde and Southsea would be an arc of a circle, and as the distance across is 4½ statute miles the centre of the arc would be 40 inches higher than the two sides; and the steamer would have ascended an inclined plane for 2¼ miles, or to the centre of the channel, and afterwards descended for the same distance towards Ryde. This ascent and descent would have been marked by the line of sight falling 40 inches nearer to the deck of the steamer when on the centre of the arc of water, as represented in the following diagram ; but as the line of sight did

not cut the steamer lower down when in the centre of the channel, and no such ascent and descent was observed, it follows necessarily that the surface of the water between Southsea and the Isle of Wight is *not convex,* and therefore the Earth as a whole is *not a globe.* The evidence against the doctrine of the Earth's rotundity is so clear and perfect, and so com*pletely* fulfils the conditions

SECTION XIII. Perspective on the Sea

required in special and independent investigations, that it is impossible for any person who can put aside the bias of previous education to avoid the opposite conclusion that the *Earth is a plam*. This conclusion is greatly confirmed by the expérience of mariners in regard to certain lighthouses. Where the light is fixed and very brilliant it can be seen at a distance, which the present doctrine of the Earth's rotundity would render altogether impossible For instance, at page 35 of "Lighthouses of the World," the Ryde Pier Light, erected in 1852, is described as a bright fixed light, 21 feet above high water, and visible from an altitude of 10 feet at the distance of 12 nautical or 14 statute miles The altitude of 10 feet would place the horizon at the distance of 4 statute miles from the observer. The square of the remaining 10 statute miles multiplied by 8 inches will give a fall or curvature downwards from the horizon of 66 feet Deduct from this 21 feet, the altitude of the light, and we have 45 feet as the amount which the light ought to be *below the horizon!*

By the same authority, at page 39, the Bidston Hill Lighthouse, near Liverpool, is 228 feet above high water, one bright fixed light, visible 23 nautical or very nearly 27 statute miles. Deducting 4 miles for the height of the observer, squaring the remaining 23 miles and multiplying that product by 8 inches we have a downward curvature of 352 feet ; from this deduct the altitude of the light, 228 feet, and there remains 124 feet as the distance which the light should be *below the horizon!*

Again, at page 40 : – "The lower light on the 'Calf of Man' is 282 feet above high water, and is visible 23 nautical miles." The usual calculation will show that it ought to be 70 feet *below the horizon !*

At page 41 the Cromer light is described as having an altitude of 274 feet above high water, and is visible 23 nautical miles, whereas it ought to be at that distance 78 feet *below the horizon !*

At page 9 it is said : – "The coal fire (which was once used) on the Spurn Point Lighthouse, at the mouth of the Humber, which was constructed on a good principle for burning, has been seen 30 miles off." If the miles here given are nautical measure they would be equal to 35 statute miles. Deducting 4 miles as the usual amount for the distance of the horizon, there will remain 31 miles, which squared and multiplied by 8 inches will give 640 feet as the declination of the water from the horizon to the base of the Lighthouse, the altitude of which is given at page 42 as 93 feet above high water. This amount deducted from the above 640 feet will leave 547 feet as the distance which the Spurn Light ought to have been *below the horizon !*

The two High Whitby Lights are 240 feet above high water (see page 42), and are visible 23 nautical miles at sea. The proper calculation will be 102 feet *below the horizon !*

At page 43, it is said that the Lower Farn Island Light is visible for 12 nautical or 14 statute miles, and the height above high water is 45 feet The usual calculation will show that this light ought to be 67 feet *below the horizon !*

The Hekkengen Light, on the west coast of Norway (see page 54), is 66 feet above high water, and visible 16 statute miles. It ought to be sunk beneath the horizon 30 feet!

The Troudhjem Light (see p. 55), on the Ringholm Rock, west coast of Norway, is 51 feet high, and is visible 16 statute miles; but ought to be 45 feet below the horizon!

The Rondo Light, also on the west coast of Norway (see p. 55), is 161 feet high, and is visible for 25 statute miles; the proper calulation will prove that it ought to be above 130 feet below the horizon!

The Egerö Light, on west point of Island, south cost of Norway (see p. 56), and which is fitted up with the first order of the dioptric lights, is visible for 28 statute miles, and the altitude above high water is 154 feet; making the usual calculation we find this light ought to be depressed, or sunk, below the horizon 230 feet!

The Dunkerque Light, on the north coast of France (see p. 71), is 194 feet high, and visible 28 statute miles. The ordinary calculation will show that it ought to be 190 feet below the horizon!

The Goulfar Bay Light, on the west coast of France, is said at page 77, to be visible 31 statute miles, and to have an altitude at high water of 276 feet, at the distance given it ought to be 210 feet below the horizon!

At page 78, the Cordonan Light, on the River Gironde, west coast of France, is given as being visible 31 statute miles, and its altitude 207 feet, which would give its depression below the horizon as nearly 280 feet!

The Light at Madras (p. 104), on the Esplanade, is 132 feet high, and visible 28 statute miles, whereas at that distance it ought to be beneath the horizon above 250 feet!

The Port Nicholson Light, in New Zealand, erected in 1859 (p. 110), is visible 35 statute miles, the altitude is 420 feet above high water, and ought, if the water is convex, to be 220 feet below the horizon!

The Light on Cape Bonavista, Newfoundland, *is 150 feet* above high water, and is visible 35 statute miles (p. 111), this will give on calculation for the Earth's rotundity, 491 feet that the Light should be below the horizon!

Many other cases could be given from the same work, shewing that the practical observations of mariners, engineers, and surveyors, entirely ignore the doctrine that the Earth is a globe. The following cases taken from miscellaneous sources will be interesting as bearing upon and leading to the same conclusion. In the *Illustrated London News* of Oct. 20, 1849, an engraving is given of a new Lighthouse erected on the Irish coast The accompanying descriptive matter contains the following sentence : – "Ballycotton Island rises 170 feet above the level of the sea ; the height of the Lighthouse is 60 feet including the Lantern ; giving the light an elevation of 230 feet, which is visible upwards of 35 miles to sea." If the 35 miles are nautical measure the distance in statute measure would be over 40 miles ; and allowing the usual distance for the horizon, there would

SECTION XIII. Perspective on the Sea

be 36 miles from thence to the Lighthouse. The square of 36 multiplied by 8 inches amounts to 864 feet; deduct the total altitude of the Lantern, 230 feet, and the remainder, 634 feet, is the distance which the Light of Ballycotton ought to be below the horizon!

In the *Times* newspaper of Monday, Oct. 16, 1854, in an account of her Majesty's visit to Great Grimsby from Hull, the following paragraph occurs: – "Their attention was first naturally directed to a gigantic tower which rises from the centre pier to the height of 300 feet, and can be seen 60 miles out at sea." The 60 miles if nautical, and this is always understood when referring to distances at sea, would make 70 statute miles, to which the fall of 8 inches belongs, and as all observations at sea are considered to be made at an elevation of 10 feet above the water, for which four miles must be deducted from the whole distance, 66 statute miles will remain, the square of which multiplied by 8 inches, gives a declination towards the tower of 2,904 feet ; deducting from this the altitude of the tower, 300 feet, we obtain the startling conclusion that the tower should be at the distance at which it is visible, (60 nautical miles,) more than 2,600 feet *below the horizon !*

The only modification which can be made or allowed in the preceding calculations is that for refraction, which is considered by surveyors generally to amount to about 1-12th of the altitude of the object observed. If we make this allowance it will reduce the various quotients *by 1-12th,* which is so little that the whole will substantially the same. Take the last tation as an instance – 2,600 feet divided 12 gives 206, which deducted from 2,600 es 2,384 as the corrected amount for action.

Note

* "Lighthouses of the World," p. 36.

SECTION 14.

GENERAL SUMMARY – APPLICATION –

CUI BONO?

IN the preceding sections it has been shown that the Copernican, or Newtonian theory of Astronomy is "an absurd composition of truth and error;" and, as admitted by its founder, "not necessarily true or even probable," and that instead of its being a general conclusion derived from known and admitted facts, it is a heterogeneous compound of assumed premises, isolated truths, and variable appearances in nature. Its advocates are challenged to show a single instance wherein a phenomenon is explained, a calculation made, or a conclusion advanced without the aid of an avowed or implied assumption ! The very construction of a theory at all, and especially such as the Copernican, is a complete violation of that natural and legitimate mode of investigation to which the term *zetetic* has been applied. The doctrine of the universality of gravita*tion* is an assumption, made only in accordance with that "pride and ambition which has led philosophers to think it beneath them to offer anything less to the world than a complete and finished system of natura." It was said, in effect, by Newton, and has ever since been insisted upon by his disciples – "Allow us, without proof, the existence of two universal forces – centrifugal and centripetal, or attraction and repulsion, and we will construct a system which shall explain all the leading mysteries of nature. An apple falling from a tree, or a stone rolling downwards, and a pail of water tied to a string set in rapid motion were assumed to be types of the relations existing among all the bodies in the universe. The moon was assumed to have a tendency to fall towards the Earth, and the Earth and Moon together towards the Sun. The same relation was assumed to exist between all the smaller and larger luminaries in the firmament ; and it soon became necessary to extend this assumption to infinity. The universe was parcelled out into systems – co-existent and illimitable. Suns, Planets, Satellites, and Comets were assumed to exist, infinite in number and boundless in extent ; and to enable the theorists to explain the alternating and constantly recuring phenomena which were everywhere observable, these numberless and for-ever-extending objects were assumed to be spheres. The Earth we inhabit was called a *planet;* and because it was thought to be reasonable that the luminous objects in the firmament which were called *planets* were *spherical* and had *motion,* so it was only reasonable to suppose that as the Earth was a planet it must also be spherical and have motion – *ergo,* the Earth is a globe, and moves upon axes and in an orbit round the Sun ! And as the Earth is a globe, and is inhabited, so again it is only reasonable to conclude that the planets are worlds like the Earth, and are inhabited by sentient beings ! What reasoning ! Assumption upon assumption, and the conclusion derived therefrom called a thing proved, to be

SECTION XIV. General Summary – Application – "CUI BONO"

employed as a truth to substantiate the first assumption ! Such a "juggle and jumble" of fancies and falsehoods, extended and intensified as it is in theoretical astronomy, is calculated to make the unprejudiced inquirer revolt in horror from the terrible conjuration which has been practised upon him ; to sternly resolve to resist its further progress ; to endeavour to overthrow the entire edifice, and to bury in its ruins the false honours which have been associated with its fabricators, and which still attach to its devotees. For the learning, the patience, the perseverance, and devotion for which they have ever been examples, honour and applause need not be withheld ; but *their* false reasoning, the advantages they have taken of the general ignorance of mankind in respect to astronomical subjects, and the unfounded theories they have advanced and defended, cannot but be regretted, and ought to be resisted. It has become a duty, paramount and imperative, to meet them in open, avowed, and unyielding rebellion ; to declare that their unopposed reign of error and confusion is over ; and that henceforth, like a falling dynasty, they must shrink and disappear, leaving the throne and the kingdom to those awakening intellects whose numbers are constantly increasing, and whose march is rapid and irresistible. The soldiers of truth and reason have drawn the sword, and ere another generation has been educated, will have forced the usurper to abdicate. The axe is lifted – it is falling, and in a very few years will have "cut the cumberer down."

The Earth a Globe, and it is necessarily demanded that it has a diurnal and an annual and various other motions ; for a globular world without motion would be useless – day and night, winter and summer, the half year's light and darkness at the "North Pole," and other phenomena could not be explained by the supposition of rotundity without the assumption also of rapid and constant motion. Hence it is *assumed* that the Earth and Moon, and all the Planets and their Satellites move in relation to each other, and that the whole move together in different planes round the Sun. The Sun and its "system" of revolving bodies are now assumed to have a general and all-inclusive motion, in common with an endless series of other Suns and systems, around some other and "central Sun" which has been assumed to be the true axis and centre of the Universe ! These assumed general motions with the particular and peculiar motions which are assigned to the various bodies in detail, together constitute a system so confused and complicated that it is almost impossible and always difficult of comprehension by the most active and devoted minds. The most simple and direct experiments, however, may be shown to prove that the Earth has no progressive motion whatever ; and here again the advocates of this interminable and entangling arrangement are challenged to produce a single instance of so called proofs of these motions which does not involve an assumption – often a glaring falsehood – but always a point which is not, or cannot be demonstrated.

The magnitudes, distances, velocities, and periodic times which these assumed motions eliminate, are all glaringly fictitious, because they are only such as a false theory creates a *necessity for*. It is geometrically demonstrable that all the visible luminaries in the firmament are within a distance of a few thousand miles, not more than the space which stretches between the North Pole and the Cape of Good Hope ; and the principle of measurement – that of plane triangulation – which demonstrates this important fact, is one which no mathematician, demanding to be considered a master in the science, dare for a moment deny. All these luminaries then, and the Sun itself, being so near to us, cannot be other than very small as compared with the Earth we inhabit They are all in motion over the Earth, which is alone immoveable, and therefore they cannot be anything more than secondary and subservient structures, ministering to this fixed material world, and to its inhabitants. This is a plain, simple, and in every respect demonstrable philosophy, agreeing with the evidence of our senses, borne out by every fairly instituted experiment, and never requiring a violation of those principles of investigation which the human mind has ever recognized, and depended upon in its every day life. The modern, or Newtonian Astronomy, has none of these characteristics. The whole system taken together constitutes a most monstrous absurdity. It is false in its foundation ; irregular, unfair, and illogical in its details ; and in its conclusions inconsistent and contradictory. Worse than all, it is a prolific source of irreligion and of atheism, of which its advocates are, practically, supporters! By defending a system which is directly opposite to that which is taught in connection with all religions, they lead the more critical and daring intellects to reject the scriptures altogether, to ignore the worship, and doubt and deny the existence of a Supreme Ruler of the world. Many of the primest minds are thus irreparably injured, robbed of those present pleasures, and that cheering hope of the future which the earnest Christian devotee holds as of far greater value than all earthly wealth and grandeur ; or than the mastery of all the philosophical complications which the human mind ever invented.

The doctrine of the Earth's rotundity and motion is now shown to be unconditionally false ; and therefore the scriptures which assert the contrary, are, in their philosophical teachings at least, *literally true.* In practical science therefore, atheism and denial of scriptural authority have no foundation. If human theories are cast aside, and the facts of nature, and legitimate reasoning alone depended upon, it will be seen that religion and true philosophy are not antagonistic, and that the hopes which both encourage may be fully relied upon. To the religious mind this matter is most important, it is indeed no less *than a* sacred question, for it renders complete the evidence that the Jewish and Christian scriptures are true, and must have been communicated to mankind by an anterior and supernal Being. For if after so many ages of mental struggling, of speculation and trial, and change and counterchange, we have at length discovered that all astronomical theories are false, that the Earth is a plane, and motionless, and that the various luminaries above it are lights only and not worlds ; and that these very doctrines have been taught and recorded in a work which has been handed down to us from the earliest times ; from a time, in fact,

SECTION XIV. General Summary – Application – "CUI BONO"

when mankind could not have had sufficient experience to enable them to criticise and doubt, much less to invent, it follows that whoever dictated and caused such doctrines to be recorded and preserved to all future generations, must have been superhuman, omniscient, and, to the Earth and its inhabitants pre-existent

To the dogged Atheist, whose "mind is made up" not to enter into any further investigation, and not to admit of possible error in his past conclusions, this question is of no more account than it is to an Ox. He who cares not to reexamine from time to time his state of mind, and the result of his accumulated experience is in no single respect better than the lowest animal in creation. He may see nothing higher, more noble, more intelligent or beautiful than himself; and in this his pride, conceit, and vanity find an incarnation. To such a creature there is no God, for he is himself an equal with the highest being he has ever recognised ! Such Atheism exists to an alarming extent among the philosophers of Europe and America ; and it has been mainly fostered by the astronomical and geological theories of the day. Besides which, in consequence of the differences between the language of Scripture and the teachings of modem Astronomy, there is to be found in the very hearts of Christian and Jewish congregations a sort of "smouldering scepticism;" a kind of faint suspicion which causes great numbers to manifest a cold and visible indifference to religious requirements. It is this which has led thousands to desert the cause of earnest, active Christianity, and which has forced the majority of those who still remain in the ranks of religion to declare "that the Scriptures were not intended to teach correctly other than moral and religious doctrines ; that the references so often made to the physical world, and to natural phenomena generally, are given in language to suit the prevailing notions and the ignorance of the people." A Christian philosopher who wrote almost a century ago in reference to remarks similar to *the above,* says, "Why should we suspect that Moses, Joshua, David, Solomon, and the later prophets and inspired writers have counterfeited their sentiments concerning the order of the universe, from pure complaisance, or being in any way obliged to dissemble with a view to gratify the prepossessions of the populace ? These eminent men being kings, lawgivers, and generals themselves, or always privileged with access to the courts of sovereign princes, besides the reverence and awful dignity which the power of divination and working of miracles procured to them, had great worldly and spiritual authority. . . They had often in charge to command, suspend, revert, and otherwise interfere with the course and laws of nature, and were never daunted to speak out the truth before the most mighty potentates on earth, much less would they be overawed by the *vox populi."* To say that the Scriptures were not intended to teach science truthfully, is in substance to declare that God himself has stated, and commissioned His prophets to teach things which are utterly false ! Those Newtonian philosophers who still hold that the sacred volume is the Word of God, are thus placed in a fearful dilemma How can the two systems, so directly opposite in character, be reconciled ? Oil and water alone will not combine – mix them by violence as we may, they will again separate when allowed to rest. Call oil oil, and water water, and acknowledge them to be distinct in nature and value ; but let no "hodge-podge" be attempted, and passed off as a genuine compound of oil and water. Call Scripture the Word of God – the Creator and Ruler of all things, and the Fountain of all Truth ; and call the Newtonian or Copernican Astronomy the word and work of man, of man, too, in his vainest mood – so vain and conceited as not to be content with the direct and simple teachings of his Maker, but who must rise up in rebellion and conjure into existence a fanciful complicated fabric, which being insisted upon as true, creates and necessitates the dark and horrible interrogatives – Is God a deceiver ? Has He spoken direct and unequivocal falsehood? Can we no longer indulge in the beautiful and consoling thought that God's justice, and love, and truth are unchanging and reliable for ever ? Let Christians – for Sceptics and Atheists may be left out of the question – to whatever division of the Church they belong, look at this matter calmly and earnestly. Let them determine to uproot the deception which has led them to think that they can altogether ignore the plainest astronomical teaching of Scripture, and endorse a system to which it is in every sense opposed. The following language is quoted as an instance *of the* manner in which the doctrine of the Earth's rotundity and the plurality of worlds interferes with Scriptural teachings: – "The theory of original sin is confuted (by our astronomical and geological knowledge), and I cannot permit the belief, when I know that our world is but a mere speck, a perishable atom in the vast space of creation, that God should just select this little spot to descend upon and assume our form, and clothe Himself in our flesh, to become visible to human eyes, to the tiny beings of this comparatively insignificant world. . . . . . Thus millions of distant worlds, with the beings allotted to them, were to be extirpated and destroyed in consequence of the original sin of Adam. No sentiment of the human mind can surely be more derogatory to the Divine attributes of the Creator, nor more repugnant to the known economy of the celestial bodies. For in the first place, who is to say, among the infinity of worlds, whether Adam was the *only creature* who was tempted by Satan and fell, and by his fall involved all the other worlds in his guilt."* The difficulty experienced by the author of the above remarks is clearly one which can no longer exist, when it is seen that the doctrine of a plurality of worlds is an impossibility. That it is an impossibility is shown by the fact that the Sun, Moon, and Stars are very small bodies, and very near to the earth ; this fact is proved by actual non-theoretical measurement; this measurement is made on the principle of plane trignometry : this principle of plane trignometry is adopted because the Earth is a Plane ; and all the base lines employed in the triangulation are horizontal By the same practical method of reasoning, all the difficulties which, upon geological and astronomical grounds, have been raised to the literal teachings of the scriptures, may be completely destroyed. Instances: – The scriptures repeatedly declare that

SECTION XIV. General Summary – Application – "CUI BONO"

the Sun moves over the Earth – "His going forth is from the end of the heaven, and his circuit unto the ends of it." "He ariseth and goeth down, and hasteth to his place whence he arose." "The sun stood still in the midst of heaven." "Great is the Earth, high is the heaven, swift is the Sun in his course." In the religious poems of all ages the same fact is presented. Christians especially, of every denomination, are familiar with, and often read and sing with delight such poetry as the following : –

> "My God who makes the Sun to know
> His proper hour to rise,
> And to give light to all below
> Doth send him *round the skies.*"

> "When from the chambers of the east
> His *morning race* begins,
> He never tires *nor stops to rest,*
> But round the world he shines."

> "God of the morning, at whose voice,
> The cheerful sun makes haste to rise,
> And, like a giant, doth rejoice,
> To run *his journey through the skies.*"

> "He sends the sun *his circuit round,*
> To cheer the fruits and warm the ground."

> "How fair has the day been!
> How bright was the Sun!
> How lovely and joyful
> The *course that he run.*"

All the expressions of scripture are consistent with the fact of the Sun's motion. They never declare anything to the contrary. Whenever they speak of the subject it is in the same manner. The direct evidence of our senses confirms it ; and actual and special observations, as well as the most practical scientific experiments, declare the same thing. The progressive and concentric motion of the Sun over the Earth is in every sense demonstrable; yet the Newtonian astronomers insist upon it that the Sun does not really move, that it only *appears* to move, and that this appearance arises from the motion of the Earth ; that when, as the scriptures affirm, the "Sun stood still in the midst of heaven,' it was the *Earth* which stood still and *not* the Sun ! that the scriptures therefore speak falsely, and the experiments of science, and the observations and applications of our senses are never to be relied upon. Whence comes this bold and arrogant denial of the value of our senses and judgement, and the authority of scripture ? The Earth or the Sun moves. Our senses tell us, and the scriptures declare that the Earth is fixed and that it is the Sun which moves above and around it ; but a *theory*, which is absolutely false in its groundwork, and ridiculously illogical in its details, demands that the Earth is round and moves upon axes, and in several other and various directions; and that these motions are *sufficient to account for* certain phenomena without supposing that the Sun moves, *therefore* the Sun is a fixed body, and his motion is *only apparent!* Such *reasoning* is a disgrace to philosophy, and fearfully dangerous to the religious interests of humanity !

Christian ministers and commentators find it a most unwelcome task when called upon to reconcile the plain and simple philosophy of the scriptures with the monstrous teachings of theoretical astronomy. Dr. Adam Clark, in a letter to the Rev. Thomas Roberts, of Bath,* speaking of the progress of his commentary, and of his endeavours to reconcile the statements of scripture with the modem astronomy, says: "Joshua's Sun and Moon standing still, have kept me going for nearly three weeks ! That one chapter has afforded me more vexation than anything I have ever met with; and even now I am but about half satisfied with my own solution of all the difficulties, though I am confident that I have removed mountains that were never touched before ; shall I say that I am heartily weary of my work, so weary that I have a thousand times wished I had never written one page of it, and am repeatedly purposing to give it up."

The Rev. John Wesley, in his journal, writes as follows: – "The more I consider them the more I doubt of all systems of astronomy. I doubt whether we can with certainty know either the distance or magnitude of any star in the firmament ; else why do astronomers so immensely differ, even with regard to the distance of the Sun from the Earth ? Some affirming it to be only three and others ninety millions of miles."*

In vol. 3, page 203, the following entry occurs: – "January 1st, 1765. – This week I wrote an answer to a warm letter published in the *London Magazine,* the author whereof is much displeased that I presume to doubt of the ' modem astronomy.' I cannot help it Nay, the more I consider the more my doubts increase; so that at present I doubt whether any man on earth knows either the distance or magnitude, I will not say of a fixed Star, but Saturn or Jupiter – yea of the Sun or Moon."

In vol. 13, page 359, he says: – "And so the whole hypothesis of innumerable Suns and worlds moving round them vanishes into air." And again at page 430 of same volume, the following words occur: – "The planets revolutions we are. acquainted with, but who is able to this day, regularly to demonstrate either their magnitude or their distance ? Unless he will prove, as is the usual way, the magnitude from the distance, and the distance from the magnitude. * * * Dr. Rogers has evidently demonstrated that no conjunction of the centrifugal and centripetal forces can possibly account for this, or even cause any body to move in an elipsis." There are several other incidental remarks to

SECTION XIV. General Summary – Application – "CUI BONO"

be found in his writings which shew that the Rev. John Wesley was well acquainted with the then modern astronomy ; and that he saw clearly both its self-contradictory and its anti-scriptural character.

It is a very popular idea among modem astronomers that the stellar universe is an endless congeries of systems, of Suns and attendant worlds peopled with sentient beings analogous in the purpose and destiny of their existence to the inhabitants of this earth. This doctrine of a plurality of worlds, although it conveys the most magnificent ideas of the universe, is purely fanciful, and may be compared to the "dreams *of the* alchemists" who laboured with unheard of enthusiasm to discover the "philosopher's stone," the *elixir vitæ,* and the "universal solvent" However grand the first two projects might have been in their realisation, it is known that they were never developed in a practical sense, and the latter idea of a solvent which would dissolve everything was suddenly and unexpectedly destroyed by the few remarks of a simple but critical observer, who demanded to know what service a substance would be to them which would dissolve all things? What could they keep it in ? for it would dissolve every vessel wherein they sought to preserve it ! This idea of a plurality of worlds is but a natural and reasonable conclusion drawn from the doctrine of the Earth's rotundity. But this doctrine being false its off shoot is equally so. The supposition that the heavenly bodies are Sun's and inhabited worlds is demonstrably impossible in nature, and has no foundation whatever in Scripture. "In the beginning God created the Heaven and *the Earth."* One Earth *only* is created ; and the fact is more especially described in Genesis, ch. i., v. 10. Where, instead of the word "Earth" meaning both land and water as together forming a globe, as it does in the Newtonian astronomy, only the *dry land* was called *earth,"* and "the gathering together of the waters called He seas." The Sun, Moon, and Stars are described as lights only and not worlds. A great number of passages might be quoted which prove that no other material world is ever in the slightest manner referred to by the sacred writers. The creation of the world ; the origin of evil, and the Ml of man ; the plan of redemption by the death of Christ ; the day of judgement, and the final consummation of all things are invariably associated with *this Earth alone.* The expression in Hebrews, ch. i, v. 2, "by whom also he made the *worlds,"* and in Heb., ch. ii., v. 3, "through faith we understand that the *worlds* were framed," are known to he a comparatively recent rendering from the original Greek documenta The word which has been translated *worlds* is fully as capable of being rendered in the singular number as the plural ; and previous to the introduction of the Copernican Astronomy was always translated *"the world."* The Roman Catholic and the French Protestant Bibles still contain the singular number ; and in a copy of an English Protestant Bible printed in the year 1608, the following translation is given : – "Through faith we understand that *the world* was ordained." So that either the plural expression "worlds" was used in later translations to accord with the astronomical notions then recently introduced, or it was meant to include *the Earth* and the spiritual world, as referred to *in*: –

Hebrews ii., 5 – *"For* unto angels hath he not put into subjection *the world to come."*

Ephesians i., 21 – "Far above all principality and power, and might, and dominion, and every name that is named not only in *this world,* but also in *that which is to come."*

Luke xviii., 29, 30 – "There is no man that hath left house, or parents, or brethren, or wife, or children, for the kingdom of God's sake, who shall not receive manifold more in this *present time,* and in *the world to come* life everlasting."

Matthew xii, 32 – "Whosoever speaketh against the Holy Ghost, it shall not he forgiven him, neither in *this world* neither in the *world to come."*

The Scriptures teach that in the day of the Lord "the Heavens shall pass away with a great noise; and the elements shall melt with fervent heat," and the "stars of Heaven fall unto the Earth even as a fig tree casteth her untimely figs when shaken of a mighty wind." The Newtonian system of astronomy declares that the stars and planets are mighty worlds – nearly all of them much larger than this Earth. The fixed stars are considered to be suns, equal to if not greater than our own sun, which is said to he above 800,000 miles in diameter. All this is proveably false, but to those who have been led to believe it, the difficult question arises, – "How can thousands of stars fall upon the Earth, which is many times less than any one of them?" How can the Earth with a supposed diameter of 8000 miles receive the numerous suns of the firmament many of which are said to he a million miles in diameter ?

These stars are assumed to have positions so far from the Earth that the distance is almost inexpressible; figures indeed may he arranged on paper but in reading them no practical idea is conveyed to the mind. Many of them are said to be so distant that should they fall with the velocity of light or above one hundred and sixty thousand miles in a second, or six hundred millions of miles per hour, they would require nearly two millions of years to reach the Earth ! Sir William Herschel in a paper on "The power of telescopes to penetrate into space," published in the *Philosophical Transactions* for the year 1800, affirms, that with his powerful instruments he discovered brilliant luminaries so far from the Earth that the light from them "could not have been less than *one million nine hundred thousand years* in *its progress."* Again the difficulty presents itself – "If the stars of Heaven begin to fall to-day, and with the greatest imaginable velocity, millions of years must elapse before they reach the Earth!" *But the*

SECTION XIV. General Summary – Application – "CUI BONO"

Scriptures declare that these changes shall occur suddenly – shall come, indeed, "as a thief in the night."

The same theory, with its false and inconceivable distances and magnitudes, operates to destroy all the ordinary, common sense, and scripturally authorised chronology. Christian and Jewish commentators, unless astronomically educated, hold and teach that the Earth, as well as the Sun, Moon, and Stars, were created about 4,000 years before the birth of Christ, or less than 6,000 years before the present time. But if many of these luminaries are so distant that their light would require above a million of years to reach us; and if, as we are taught, bodies are visible to us because of the light which they reflect or radiate, then their light *has* reached us, because we have been able to see them, and therefore they must have been shining, and must have been created at least *one million nine hundred thousand years ago*! The chronology of the bible indicates that a period of six thousand years has not yet elapsed since "the Heavens and the Earth were finished, and *all* the Host of them."

In the modern astronomy, Continents, Oceans, Seas, and Islands, are considered as together forming one vast Globe of 25,000 miles in circumference. This has been shown to be fallacious, and it is clearly contrary to the plain, literal teaching of the scriptures. In the first chapter of Genesis, we find the following language: "and God said let the waters under the heaven be gathered unto one place, and let the *dry land* appear ; and it was so. And God called the dry land *Earth,* and the gathering together of the waters called He Seas." Here the Earth and Seas – Earth and the great body of waters, are described as two distinct and independent regions, and not as together forming one Globe which astronomers call "the Earth." This description is confirmed by several other passages of scripture.

2 Peter, iii., 5 – "For this they willingly are ignorant of, that by the Word of God the Heavens were of old, and the Earth *standing out of the waters and in the waters."*

Psalms cxxxvi., 6 – "O give thanks to the Lord of Lords, that by wisdom made the heavens, and that *stretchet out the earth above the waters."*

Psalms xxiv., 1, 2 – "The earth is the Lord's and the fulness thereof ; the world and they that dwell therein : for he hath *founded it upon the seas, and established it upon the floods."*

Hermes (New Testament Apocrypha) – "Who with the word of his strength fixed the heaven; and *founded the earth upon the waters."*

Job xxvi., 7 – "He stretcheth out the north over the empty place, and hangeth the Earth upon nothing."

Some think that the latter part of this verse, "hangeth the Earth upon nothing," favours the idea that the Earth is a globe revolving in space without visible support; but Dr. Adam Clark, although himself a Newtonian philosopher, says, in his commentary upon this passage in Job, the literal translation is, "on the hollow or empty waste," and he quotes a Chaldee version of the passage which runs as follows : "He layeth the Earth upon the waters nothing sustaining it."

It is not that He "hangeth the Earth upon nothing," but "hangeth or layeth it upon the waters" which were empty or waste, and where before there was nothing. This is in strict accordance with the other expressions, that "the Earth was founded upon the waters," &c., and also with the expression in Genesis, "that the face of the deep was covered only with darkness."

If the Earth were a globe, it is evident that everywhere the water of its surface, the seas, lakes, oceans, and rivers, must he sustained by the land, the Earth must be under the water ; hut if the land and the waters are distinct, and the Earth is "founded upon the seas," then everywhere the sea must sustain the land as it does a ship or any other floating mass, and there is water below the earth. In this particular as in all the others, the scriptures are beautifully sequential aud consistent

Exodus xx, 4 – "Thou shalt not make unto thee any likeness of anything in heaven above or in the Earth beneath, or in the *waters under the Earth."*

Genesis xliv, 25 – "The Almighty shall bless thee with the blessings of heaven above, and blessings of the *deep that lieth under."*

Deut. xxxiii, 13 – "Blessed be his land, for the precious things of heaven ; for the dew ; and for the *deep which couched beneath."*

Deut. iv, 18 – "Take ye therefore good heed unto yourselves, and make no similitude of anything on the Earth, or the likeness of anything that is in the *waters beneath the Earth"*

The same idea prevailed among the ancients generally. In Ovid's Metamorphoses, Jupiter, in an assembly of the gods, is made to say, "I swear by the infernal *waves which glide under the Earth."*

If the earth is a distinct structure standing in and upon the waters of the "great deep," it follows that, unless it can be shown that something else sustains the waters, that the depth is fathomless. As there is no evidence whatever of anything existing underneath the "great deep," and as in many parts of the Atlantic and Pacific Oceans no bottom has been found by the most scientific and efficient means which human *ingenuity* could invent, we are forced to the conclusion that the depth is boundless. This conclusion is again confirmed by the scriptures.

Jeremiah xxxi, 37 – "Thus saith the Lord, which giveth the sun for a light by day, and the ordinances of the moon and of the stars for a light by night, which divideth the sea when the waves thereof roar, the Lord of Hosts is His name. If these ordinances depart from before me, saith the Lord, then the seed of Israel also shall cease from being a nation before me for ever. Thus saith the Lord : if heaven above can be measured, and the *foundations* of the *Earth searched out beneath,* I will also cast off all the seed of Israel."

From the above it will he seen that God's promises to his people could no more be broken than could the height of heaven, or the depths of the Earth's

SECTION XIV. General Summary – Application – "CUI BONO"

foundations be searched out The fathomless deep beneath – upon which the Earth is founded, and the infinitude of heaven above, are here given as emblems of the boundlessness of God's power, and of the certainty that all his ordinances will be fulfilled. When God's power can be limited, heaven above will no longer be infinite ; and the mighty waters, the foundations of the earth may be fathomed. But the scriptures plainly teach us that the power and wisdom of God, the heights of Heaven, and the depths of the waters under the Earth, are alike unfathomable ; and no true philosophy ever avers, nor ever did nor ever can aver, a single fact to the contrary.

In all the religions of the Earth the words "up" and "above" are associated with a region of peace and happiness. Heaven is always spoken of as *above* the *Earth*. The scriptures invariable convey the same idea : –

Deut. xxvi., 15 – "Look *down* from Thy holy habitation, from Heaven, and bless Thy people Israel."

Exodus xix., 20 – "And the Lord came *down* upon Mount Sinai."

Psalm cii., 19 – "For he hath looked *down* from the height of his sanctuary: from Heaven did the Lord behold the Earth."

Isaiah lxiii., 15 – "Look *down* from Heaven, and behold from the habitation of Thy holiness and of Thy glory."

Psalm ciii., 11 – "For as the Heaven is high *above the Earth."*

2 *Kings* ii., 11 – "And Elijah went *up* by a whirlwind into Heaven."

Mark xvi., 10 – "So then after the Lord had spoken unto them he was received *up into Heaven."*

Luke xxiv., 51 – "And it came to pass, while He blessed them, He was parted from them, and c*arried up into Heaven."*

If the Earth is a globe revolving at the rate of above a thousand miles an hour all this language of scripture is necessarily fallacious. The terms "up" and "down," and "above" and "below," are words without meaning, at best are merely relative – indicative of no absolute or certain direction. That which is "up" at noon-day, is directly "down" at midnight Heaven can only be spoken of as "above," and the scriptures can only be read correctly for a single moment out of the twenty-four hours ; for before the sentence "Heaven is high above the Earth" could be uttered, the speaker would be descending from the meridian where Heaven was above him, and his eye although unmoved would be fixed upon a point millions of miles away from his first position. Hence in all the ceremonials of religion, where the hands and eyes are raised upwards to Heaven, nay when Christ himself "lifted up his eyes to Heaven and said, Father, the hour is come," his gaze would be sweeping along the firmament at rapidly varying angles, and with such incomprehensible velocity that a fixed point of observation, and a definite position, as indicating the seat or throne of "Him that sitteth in the Heavens" would be an impossibility.

Again : the religious world have always believed and meditated upon the word "Heaven" as representing an infinite region of joy and safety, of rest and happiness unspeakable; as "the place of God's residence, the dwelling place of angels and the blessed; the true palace of God, entirely separated from the impurities and imperfections, the alterations and changes of the lower world ; where He reigns in eternal peace * * It is the sacred mansion of light, and joy, and glory.*" But if there is a plurality of worlds, millions upon millions, nay, an "infinity of worlds," if the universe is filled with innumerable systems of burning suns, and rapidly revolving planets, intermingled with rushing comets and whirling satellites, all dashing and sweeping through space in directions, and with velocities surpassing all human comprehension, and terrible even to contemplate, where is the place of rest and safety? Where is the true and unchangeable "palace of God?" In what direction is Heaven to be found? Where is the liberated human soul to find its home – its refuge from change and motion, from uncertainty and danger ? Is it to wander for ever in a labyrinth of rolling worlds ? To struggle for ever in a never ending maze of revolving suns and systems? To be never at rest, but for ever seeking to avoid some vortex of attraction – some whirlpool of gravitation? The belief in the existence of Heaven, as a region of peace and harmony "extending (above the Earth) through all extent," and beyond the influence of natural laws and restless elements, is jeopardised, if not destroyed, by a false and usurping astronomy, which has no better foundation than human conceit and presumption. If this ill-founded, unsupported philosophy is admitted by the religious mind, it can no longer say that –

> "Far above the sun, and stars, and skies,
> In realms of endless light and love,
> My Father's mansion lies."

The modem theoretical astronomy affirms that the Moon is a solid opaque, non-luminous body ; that it is, in fact, nothing less than a material world. It has even been mapped out into continents, islands, seas, lakes, volcanoes, &c., &c. The nature of its atmosphere and character of its productions and possible inhabitants have been discussed with as much freedom as though our philosophers were quite as familiar with it as they are with the different objects and localities upon Earth. The light, too, with which the Moon so beautifully illuminates the firmament is declared to be only borrowed – to be only the light of the Sun intercepted and reflected upon the Earth These doctrines are not only opposed by a formidable array of well-ascertained facts (as given in previous sections), but they are totally denied by the scripture. The Sun and Moon and Stars are never referred to as worlds, but simply as *lights* to rule alternately in the firmament

Genesis i., 14, 16 – "And God said let there he *lights* in the firmament of the Heaven to divide the day from the night * * * And God made two *great lights* – the greater light to rule the day, and the lesser light to rule the night

SECTION XIV. General Summary – Application – "CUI BONO"

Psalm cxxxvi., 7, 9 – "O give thanks to Him that made *great lights* : the Sun to rule by day, the Moon and Stars to rule by night."

Jeremiah, xxxi., 35 – "The Sun is given for a light by day, and the ordinances of the Moon and of the Stars for a light by night"

Ezekiel, xxxii, 7, 8 – "I will cover the Sun with a cloud ; and the Moon shall not give *her light."* "All the bright lights of Heaven will I make dark over thee."

Psalm cxlviii., 3 – "Praise him Sun and Moon, praise him all ye Stars of light"

Isaiah xiii., 10 – "The Sun shall he darkened in his going forth, and the Moon shall not cause *her* light to shine."

Matthew xxiv, 29 – "Immediately after the tribulation of those days shall the Sun be darkened, and the Moon shall not give her light."

Isaiah ix., 19, 20 – The Sun shall be no more *thy light* by day; neither for brightness shall the *Moon give light* unto thee. * * Thy Sun shall no more go down ; neither shall thy Moon withdraw itself."

Psalm cxxxvi., 7 to 9 – "To him that made great lights, the Sun to rule by day, the Moon and Stars to rule by night."

Job xxv., 5 – "Behold even to the Moon, and *it* shineth not."

Ecclesiastes xii., 2 – "While the Sun, or the light, or the Moon, or the Stars be not darkened."

Isaiah xxx., 26 – "The light of the Moon shall be as the light of the Sun ; and the light of the Sun shall be sevenfold."

Deuteronomy xxxiii., 14 – "And for the precious fruits brought forth by the Sun, and for the preciaus things put forth by the Moon."

In the very first of the passages above quoted the doctrine is enunciated that various distinct and independent *lights* were created. But that two *great* lights were specially called into existence for the purpose of ruling the day and the night. The Sun and the Moon are declared to be these great and alternately ruling lights. Nothing is here said, nor is it in any other part of scripture said, that the Sun is a great light, and that the Moon shines only by reflection. The Sun is called the "greater light to rule the day," and the Moon the "lesser light to rule the night." Although of these two "great lights" one is less than the other, each is declared to shine with its own light Hence in Deuteronomy, c. 33, v. 14, it is affirmed that certain fruits are specially brought forth by the influence of the Sun's light, and that certain other productions are "put forth by the Moon." That the light of the sun is influential in encouraging the growth of certain natural products ; and that the light of the Moon has a distinct influence in promoting the increase of certain other natural substances, is a matter well known to those who are familiar with horticultural and agricultural phenomena ; and it is abundantly proved by chemical evidence that the two lights are distinct in character and in action upon various elements. This distinction is beautifully preserved throughout the sacred scriptures. In no single instance are the two lights confounded. On the contrary, in the New Testament, St. Paul affirms with authority, that "there is one glory of the Sun, and another glory of the Moon, and another glory of the Stars."

The same fact of the difference in the two lights, and their independence of eath other is maintained in the scriptures to the last. "The Sun became black as sackcloth of hair, and the Moon became as blood." If the Moon is only a reflector, the moment the Sun becomes black *her surface* will be blackened also, and not remain as blood, while the Sun is dark and black as sackcloth of hair !

Again : the modem system of astronomy teaches that this earth cannot possibly receive light from the Stars, because of their supposed great distance from it : that the fixed Stars are only burning spheres, or Sun's to their own systems of planets and satellites : and that their light terminates, or no longer produces an active luminosity at the distance of nearly two thousand millions of miles. Here again the scriptures affirm the contrary doctrine.

Genesis i., 16 – 17 – "He made the Stars also ; and God set them in the firmament *to give light upon the earth*."

Isaiah xiii., 10 – "For the Stars of Heaven and the constellations thereof shall not *give their light*."

Ezekiel xxxii., 7 – "I will cover the Heaven, and make the *Stars* thereof *dark.*"

Joel ii., 10 – "The Sun and the Moon shall be dark, and the *Stars* shall withdraw *their shining*."

Psalm cxlviii., 3 – "Praise him Sun and Moon : promise him all ye *Stars of Light.*"

Jeremiah xxxi., 35 – "Thus saith the Lord, which giveth the Sun for a light by day ; and the ordinances of the Moon and of *the Stars* for a li*ght by night*."

Daniel xii., 3 – "They that turn many to righteousness shall *shine* as the *Stars* for ever and ever."

These quotations place it beyond doubt that the Stars were made expressly to shine in the firmament, and "to give light upon the Earth." In addition to this language of scripture, we have the evidence of our own eyes that the Stars give abundant light "What beautiful starlight!" is a common expression : and we all remember the difference between a dark and starless night, and one when the firmament is as it were studded with brilliant luminaries. Travellers inform us that in many parts of the world, where the sky is clear and free from clouds and vapours for weeks together, the Stars appear both larger and brighter than they do in England ; and that their light is sufficiently intense to enable them to read and write, and to travel with safety through the most dangerous places.

If it be true that the Stars and the Planets are not simply lights, as the scriptures affirm them to be, but magnificent worlds, for the most part much larger than this earth, then it is a very proper question to ask – "are they inhabited?" If the answer be in the affirmative, it is equally proper to inquire "have the first parents in each world been tempted ?" If so, "have they fallen?" if so, "Have they required redemption?" And "have they been redeemed ?" "Has

SECTION XIV. General Summary – Application – "CUI BONO"

each world had a separate Redeemer ? or has Christ been the Redeemer for every world in the universe?" And if so, "did His suffering and crucifixion on this Earth suffice for the redemption of the fallen inhabitants of all other worlds ? Or had He to suffer and die in each world successively ? Did the fail of Adam in this world involve in his guilt the inhabitants of all other worlds ? Or was the baneful influence of Satan confined to the first parents of this Earth ? If so, why so ? and if not, why not ? But, and if, and why, and again – but it is useless thus to ponder ! The Christian philosopher must be confounded! If his religion be to him a living reality, he will turn with loathing or spurn with indignation and disgust, as he would a poisonous reptile, a system of astronomy which creates in his mind so much confusion and uncertainty! But as the system which necessitates such doubts and difficulties has been shown to be purely theoretical ; and to have not the slightest foundation in fact, the religious mind has really no cause for apprehension. Not a shadow of doubt remains that this World is the only one created ; that the sacred Scriptures contain, in addition to religious and moral doctrines, a true and consistent philosophy ; that they were written for the good of mankind, at the direct instigation of God himself ; and that all their teachings and promises are truthful, consistent, and reliable. Whoever holds the contrary conclusion is the victim of an arrogant false astronomy, of an equally false and presumptuous geology, or a suicidal method of reasoning – a logic which never demands μ proof of its premises, and which therefore leads to conclusions which are contrary to nature, to human experience, and to the direct teaching of God's word, and therefore contrary to the deepest and most lasting interests of humanity. "God has spoken to man in two voices, the voice of inspiration and the voice of nature. By man's ignorance they have been made to disagree ; but the time will come, and cannot be far distant, when these two languages will strictly accord ; when the science of nature will no longer contradict the science of scripture."*

CUI BONO. – "Of all terrors to the generous soul, that *Cui bono* is the one to be the most zealously avoided. Whether it be proposed to find the magnetic point, or a passage impossible to be utilised if discovered, or a race of men of no good to any human institution extant, and of no good to themselves ; or to seek the Unicorn in Madagascar, and when we had found him not to be able to make use of him ; or the great central plateau of Australia, where no one could live for centuries to come ; or the great African lake, which, for all the good it would do us English folk might as well be in the Moon ; or the source of the Nile, the triumphant discovery of which would neither lower the rents nor take off the taxes anywhere – whatever it is, the *Cui bono* is always a weak and cowardly argument : essentially short-sighted too, seeing that, according to the law of the past, by which we may always safely predicate the future, so much falls into the hands of the seeker, for which he was not looking, and of which he never even knew the existence. The area of the possible is very wide still, and very insignificant and minute, the angle we have staked out and marked impossible. What do we know of the powers which nature has yet in reserve, of the secrets she has still untold, the wealth still concealed ? Every day sees new discoveries in the sciences we can investigate at home. What, then, may not lie waiting for the explorers abroad? Weak and short-sighted commercially, the *cui bono* is worse than both, morally. When we remember the powerful manhood, the patience, unselfishness, courage, devotion, and nobleness of aim which must accompany a perilous enterprise, and which form so great an example, and so heart-stirring to the young and to the wavering, it is no return to barbaric indifference to life to say, better indeed a few deaths for even a commercially useless enterprise – better a few hearths made desolate, and a few wives and mothers left to bear their stately sorrow to the end of time, that the future may rejoice and be strong: better a thousand failures, and a thousand useless undertakings, than the loss of national manhood or the weakening of the national fibre. Quixotism is a folly when the energy which might have achieved conquests over misery and wrong, if rightfully applied, is wasted in fighting windmills ; but to forego any great enterprise for fear of the dangers attending, or to check a grand endeavour by the *cui bono* of ignorance and moral scepticism, is worse than a folly – it is baseness, and a cowardice.*"

The above quotation is an excellent general answer to all those who may, in reference to the subject of this work, or to anything which is not of immediate worldly interest, obtrude the *cui bono?* But as a special reply it may be claimed for the subject of these pages –

First, – It is more edifying, more satisfactory, and in every sense far better that we should know the true and detect the false. Thereby the mind becomes fixed, established upon an eternal foundation, and no longer subject to those waverings and changes, those oscillations and fluctuations which are ever the result of falsehood. To know the truth and to embody it in our lives and purposes our progress must be safe and rapid, and almost unlimited in extent None can say to what it may lead or where it may culminate. Who shall dare to set bounds to the capabilities of the mind, or to fix a limit to human progress ? Whatever may be the destiny of the human race truth alone will help and secure its realisation.

Second, – Having detected the fundamental falsehoods of modem astronomy, and discovered that the Earth is a plane, and motionless, and the only material world in existence, we are able to demonstrate the actual character of the Universe. In doing this we are enabled to prove that all the so-called arguments with which so many scientific but irreligious men have assailed the scriptures, are absolutely false; have no foundation except in their own astronomical and geological theories, which being demonstrably fallacious, they fall to the ground as valueless. They can no longer be weilded as weapons against religion. If used at all it can only be that their weakness and utter worthlessness will be exposed. Atheism and every other form of Infidelity are thus rendered helpless. Their sting is cut away, and their poison dissipated. The

SECTION XIV. General Summary – Application – "CUI BONO"

irreligious philosopher can no longer obtrude his theories as things proved wherewith to test the teachings of scripture. He must now himself be tested. He must be forced to demonstrate his premises, a thing which he has never yet attempted ; and if he fails in this respect his impious vanity, self-conceit, and utter disregard of justice, will become so clearly apparent that his presence in the ranks of science will no longer be tolerated. All theory must be put aside, and the questions at issue must be decided by independent and practical evidence. This has been dona The process – the *modus operandi*, and the conclusions derived therefrom have been given in the early sections of this work. They are entirely consonant with the teachings of scriptura The scriptures are therefore literally true, and must henceforth either alone or in conjunction with practical science be used as a standard by which to test the truth or falsehood of every system which does or may hereafter exist Philosophy is no longer to be employed as a test of scriptural truth, but the scriptures may and ought to be the test of all philosophy. Not that they are to be used as a test of philosophy simply because they are *thought* or *believed* to be the word of God, but because their literal teachings in regard *to* science and natural phenomena, are demonstrably correct It is quite as faulty and unjust for the religious devotee to urge the scriptures against the theories of the philosopher simply because he *believes* them to be true, as it is for the philosopher to urge his theories against the scriptures only because he disbelieves the one and believes the other. The whole matter must be taken out of the region of belief and disbelief. The Christian will be strengthened and his mind more completely satisfied by having it in his power to demonstrate that the scriptures are philosophically true, than he could possibly be by the simple belief in their validity, unsupported by practical evidence. On the other hand the Atheist who is met by the Christian upon purely scientific grounds, and who is not belaboured with enunciations of what his antagonist believes, will be led to listen and to pay more regard and respect to the reasons advanced than he could possibly concede to the purely religious argument, or to an argument founded upon faith alone. If it can be shown to the atheistical philosopher that his astronomical and geological theories are fallacious, and that all the expressions in the scriptures which have reference to natural phenomena are literally true, he will of necessity be led to admit that, apart from all other considerations, if the *philosophy* of the scriptures is demonstrably correct, then possibly their *spiritual* and *moral* teachings may also be true ; and if so, they may and indeed must have had a divine origin ; and if so they are truly the "word of God," and after all, religion is a grand reality ; and the theories which speculative adventurous philosophers have advanced are nothing better than treacherous quicksands into which many of the deepest thinkers have been engulphed and lost. By this process many highly intelligent minds have been led to desert the ranks of Atheism and to rejoin the army of Christian soldiers and devotees. Many have rejoiced almost beyond expression that the subject of the Earth's true form and position in the universe had ever been brought under their notice ; and doubtless great numbers will yet be induced to return to that allegiance which plain demonstrable truth demands and deserves. To induce numbers of earnest thinking human beings to leave the rebellious cause of Atheism and false philosophy; to return to a full recognition of the beauty and truthfulness of the scriptures, and to a participation in the joy and satisfaction which religion can alone supply, is a grand and cheering result, and one which furnishes the noblest possible answer to the ever ready "Cui Bono."

In addition to the numerous quotations which *have* been given from the sacred scriptures, and proved to be true and consistent, it may be useful briefly to refer to the following difficulties which have been raised by the scientific objectors to scriptural authority : – "As the earth is a globe, and as all its vast collections of water – its oceans, lakes, &c., are sustained by the earthy crust beneath them, and as beneath this 'crust of the earth' everything is in a red-hot molten condition to what place could the excess of waters retire which are said in the scriptures to have overwhelmed the whole world? It could not sink into the centre of the earth, for the fire is there so intense that the whole would be rapidly volatilised, and driven away as vapour. It could not evaporate, for when the atmosphere is charged with watery vapour beyond a certain degree it begins to condense and throw back the water in the form of rain ; so that the waters of the flood could not sink from the earth's surface, nor remain in the atmosphere ; therefore if the earth had ever been deluged at all, it would have remained so to this day. But as it is not universally flooded so it never could have been, and the account given in the scriptures is false." All this specious reasoning is founded upon the assumption that the earth is a globe : this doctrine, however, being false, all the difficulties quickly vanish. The earth being "founded on the seas" would be as readily cleared of its superfluous water as would the deck of a ship on emerging from a storm. Or as a rock in the ocean would be cleared after the raging waves which for a time everwhelmed it had subsided.

"Thou coveredst the Earth with the deep as with a garment ; the waters stood above the mountains. At thy rebuke they fled; and at the voice of thy thunder they hasted away. . . . down by the valleys unto the place which thou hast founded for them."*

"Thou didst cleave the Earth with rivers ; and the overflowing of the waters passed by ; and the deep uttered his voice and lifted up his hands on high."†

The surface of the Earth standing above the level of the surrounding seas, the waters of the flood would simply and naturally run down by the valleys and rivers into the "great deep," – into which "the waters returned from off the earth continually . . . until the tenth month, and on the first day of the month were the tops of the mountains seen."‡

Again ; as the Earth is a Globe and in continual motion, how could Jesus on being "taken up into an exceedingly high mountain see all the kingdoms of the world, in a moment of time ?" Or, when "He cometh with clouds and *every*

SECTION XIV. General Summary – Application – "CUI BONO"

eye shall see him," how could it be possible, seeing that at least twenty-four hours would elapse before every part of the Earth would bo turned to the same point? But it has been demonstrated that the Earth is a Plane and motionless, and that from a great eminence every part of its surface could be seen at once ; and, at once – at the same moment, could every eye behold Him, when "coming in a cloud with power and great glory."

Notes

* Encyclopædia Londenensis, p. 457, vol. 2.
* Life of Adam Clark, 8vo Edition.
* Extracts from works of Rev. J. Wesley, 3rd Edition, 1829. Published by Mason, London, p. 392, vol. 2.
* Cruden's Concordance, article "Heaven."
* Professor Hunt.
* *Daily News* of April 5, 1865.
* *Psalm civ.*
† Hab. iii. 9-10.
‡ Gen. viii. 2-5.

FINIS.

S. HAYWARD, PRINTER, GREEN STREET, BATH.

www.ingramcontent.com/pod-product-compliance
Lightning Source LLC
Chambersburg PA
CBHW071305040426
42444CB00009B/1883